Archaeology and the Biblical Record

Bernard Alpert
and
Fran Alpert

HAMILTON BOOKS

A member of
THE ROWMAN & LITTLEFIELD PUBLISHING GROUP
Lanham • Boulder • New York • Toronto • Plymouth, UK

Library of Congress Control Number: 2011946152
ISBN: 978-0-7618-5835-5 (paperback : alk. paper)
eISBN: 978-0-7618-5836-2

Cover image depicts spies returning from Canaan bearing fruits of the Land of Milk and Honey. The Israelites reject their minority report, causing them to wander an additional forty years in the wilderness (Numbers 13 and 14).

∞™ The paper used in this publication meets the minimum requirements of American National Standard for Information Sciences—Permanence of Paper for Printed Library Materials, ANSI Z39.48-1992

"When I have a difficult subject before me. . . . [and] can see no other way of teaching a well-established truth except by pleasing one intelligent man and displeasing ten thousand fools, I prefer to address myself to one man and take no notice whatever of the condemnation of the multitude."

Moses Maimonides,
Moreh Nevuchim: The Guide for the Perplexed

Contents

List of Figures

Acknowledgments

We are grateful for the hard work and efforts of archaeologists and Biblical scholars who have, over the recent past, accumulated knowledge that has allowed us to formulate this book; in particular, we acknowledge Israel Finkelstein, Neil Asher Silberman, Richard Elliott Friedman, William G. Dever, James L. Kugel, and Michael Fishbane, along with many others. It is our hope that readers will turn to their research for further study and enlightenment.

We also extend thanks to:
Karen Stang Hanley, our editor, who helped us through the myriad details associated with publishing. Her calm yet enthusiastic guidance has propelled this work to fruition.

Dr. Ian Stern and Heidi Stern, valued long-time colleagues and friends.

Professor Amos Kloner, who mentored us during our early years at Tel Maresha.

Julia Filipone Erez, a creative artist and our talented illustrator.

Dr. Betsy Katz and Michael Katz for acting as our sounding boards.

Our Bible Study Group, whose members have contributed to our knowledge for more than 35 years.

Michael Hoffman and Daniel Alpert of See3 Marketing for their expertise.

Dr. Norman Enteen, Dr. Ted Miller, Barry and Jill Levenfeld, Peter Halban, the staff of the Institute of Archaeology, Oxford, for their inspiration and encouragement.

Iris, Abby, Andrea and Chava Alpert, Dr. Gerald Selvin and Michael Bloom for their early commitment to this endeavor and their continued support.

Several translations of the Biblical text were used and an effort was made to preserve the essence of the work.

Historical Time
Periods according to the Bible*

Middle Bronze Age 1850–1550 BCE
  1850–1750 Age of the Patriarchs and Matriarchs
  1750–1550 Hyksos Invasions and Rule in Egypt

Late Bronze Age 1550–1200 BCE
  El Amarna Period; Exodus and Revelation at Sinai; emergence of the Israelite people

Israelite Period 1200–586 BCE
  Iron Age I 1200–980 BCE
    1200–980 Judges; Philistine invasion
  Iron Age II 1020–722 BCE
    1020–980 United Monarchy: Saul, David and Solomon
    980–722 Divided Monarchy; fall of Israel to Assyrians
  Iron Age III 8th century–586 BCE
    722–586 Kingdom of Judah; period of Classical Prophets
    586 Fall of Judah; Jews exiled to Babylon

Babylonian Period and Persian Period 586–322 BCE
  Persian rule; Exiles return to Judea; Second Temple completed
  Ezra and Nehemiah; Alexander conquers Judea; Maccabean War
  Hanukkah

Hasmonean and Herodian Period 167 BCE–70 CE
  Hasmonean rule; Roman rule; Herod enlarges Second Temple

Beginnings of Christianity; Jewish revolt leads to destruction of Jerusalem and the Temple

Note: Most dates are approximate except those after the 7th century BCE, when events can be confirmed by outside (non-Biblical) sources.

Introduction

The dramatic story of the Israelite people spans Abraham's journey from Mesopotamia to Canaan; the deliverance from slavery; the wandering in the desert and the Revelation at Sinai; the emergence of the Israelite people in Canaan; and the rise and fall of the early monarchy followed by the destruction of the Northern Kingdom. Despite their familiarity, however, these events did not occur as they are described in the corresponding five books of the Bible.

So why re-scrutinize that same Bible which has nourished and sustained humankind for a millennium? The Biblical narrative has been explored repeatedly by theologians, historians, and Biblical archaeologists. The revisionists and minimalists (those who disclaim the traditional Biblical account) in the area of Biblical studies have been challenged by a broad spectrum of both Jewish and Christian lay teachers. However, the latest interpretation of Biblical events in relation to archaeological studies has not made an impact on the teaching of mainstream established religion. We have not succeeded in engaging our youth in the reality of what the Biblical narrative represents; instead we leave them with oversimplified and often incorrect answers. We avoid serious and honest confrontation with the Biblical text.

At the same time, fundamentalists of all faiths are still insisting on the truth of the Biblical creation text nearly 150 years after Darwin and almost 90 years after the Scopes trial. Intelligent design and creationism are recent and widely popular responses to the theory of evolution. In fact, some believe that if the theory of evolution is accepted, Israel will lose its right to the land of Israel. The archaeological record shows that the Israelite nation began to coalesce by approximately 1200 BCE, establishing itself as an autonomous kingdom around 1000 BCE. This dating confirms Israel's right to the territory of the state of Israel 1000 years before Christianity, and 1600 years before Islam.

According to the archaeological record, the history of the Jewish people prior to the 8th to 7th century BCE that is described in the Bible may have happened, but the sequence of events was probably different. From the Middle Bronze Age to Iron Age II the narrative was rewritten by revisionists over a relatively short period of time, in order to give the Israelites a cohesive and exciting narrative aimed at shaping their national identity. The issue of a God concept is not altered or denied by this archaeological evidence; only the time frame of its development is reconsidered. "The Bible's value lies not in its historical accuracy, but rather in the religious and theological truths it conveys through the use of narratives, laws, wisdom-literature and prophecy" (Levine 1995).

There have been many attempts to refute the authority of the Bible. Biblical criticism, when it developed in the 19th century, attempted to show that the Bible was written by a series of editors and redactors (those who selected, abridged and combined text from earlier manuscripts to produce the Biblical narrative). These theories were disparaged by traditional Biblical scholars and theologians, who defended the Bible as a more authentic and historical document that was divinely received at Sinai and accepted by Jews, Christians, and Muslims. No proof can be presented that will dishearten these "believers." The actual archaeological evidence discussed in these pages cannot be wished or washed away, and our purpose is to enlighten the open-minded reader to see that "It Ain't Necessarily So!"

Faith is based on feelings, which are emotional and personal, while thoughts or ideas are grounded in rational truth, and must be freshly considered upon the discovery of new evidence. This does not mean that religious faith falls by the wayside when juxtaposed with archaeological evidence. Quite the opposite! It is possible to honor more than one truth. The interface between religion and archaeology need not be adversarial. Instead, this meeting can serve as a basis for creating new understandings of the Biblical text as well as the archaeological evidence.

Archaeology is an objective, scientific discipline that explains and describes human society, using artifacts and the cultural landscape. Its findings are based on logical argument, the use of hypothesis, and comparative models which are continually being tested. Archaeology does not always produce conclusive evidence. However, excavations in Israel and the Sinai Desert create an objective historical sequence that is difficult to dispute. Up until the mid-20th century, there was much misinterpretation of the archaeological evidence by early practitioners who were overcome by their own theological inclinations. The idea of Biblical archaeology is no longer considered a major factor in the archaeological discipline. The excavations that have taken place over the past 50 years conclusively confirm that the narrative of the Bible and the history of ancient Israel are not parallel; in fact, they only begin to interface or correspond in the 8th and 7th centuries BCE, nearly 1,000 years after the earliest events described in the Biblical account.

The Bible continues to be recognized as a work of great literary and spiritual genius, but we must acknowledge that the historical record is separate and clear. Although it is difficult to edit a story that has been written with our "mother's milk," the truth must be known. It is intellectually unacceptable to perpetuate from generation to generation the Biblical narrative as if it were strictly factual.

It is important to remember, however, that the story does not have to change, only our perception of it. This is the challenge for Biblical scholars and those who work in religious education. They are the ones who must find a forum that is intellectually and emotionally ready to confront these issues lest the Bible stories be relegated to mere myth.

This book is intended to be popular literature for the general public, accessible to anyone who is interested in making the Bible meaningful to the 21st century. It is for those thoughtful readers who are willing to accept the fact that what we were taught by our parents and teachers is not the truth as we know it today. They taught us what they believed was divine revelation, which they learned in turn from their elders. It was a continuation of an oral tradition that did not have the opportunity to be informed by the archaeological record.

We do not wish to rewrite the history of Biblical Israel. Rather, we want to reinforce a historical and verifiable understanding of what took place in the 8th and 7th centuries BCE, and, as a result, increase our understanding of how our perception of the five books of the Torah (as well as Joshua, Judges, Kings, and Chronicles) should change, based on the archaeological evidence. This an ongoing process in which there are still questions to be answered. There may never be a final and definitive account, since archaeology is a continuing process.

What prevents educated thinkers from examining the Bible as they would any other text, whether fact or fiction? There are several issues at work: the aura of the holiness of the text, concern about tampering with tradition, the fear that change will in some way condemn the scholar to purgatory, and for many, just plain denial. Those who might otherwise become religious adherents are put off by this lack of openness. In this volume we seek to give the perplexed layman, young or old, Jewish, Christian, or Muslim, a new understanding of the Bible and how it is illuminated by the archaeological record. It is hoped that the reader will then be able to integrate this critical approach into a richer modern world view.

We have so much more information than our forefathers had when the Bible was codified. No doubt the early redactors would have embraced all the new perspectives that are now readily available. If they had known of these recent archaeological findings, the traditional narrative would have been different. The challenge now is to examine the Biblical narrative and open it to definitive archaeological finds, blending the two to deepen and preserve our rich heritage.

Chapter One

Archaeology
Biblical and Modern Archaeology

Modern archaeology now offers the best way of dealing objectively with interpretations and theories that were often contaminated by personal prejudices in the early development of the practice of archaeology. The discipline of Biblical archaeology, the study of material remains that are contemporaneous with the events described in the Bible, strives to link the finds with the events; however, this aspect of archaeology no longer enjoys the same respectability as it did in the mid-20th century. Archaeological findings, while still subject to interpretation and disagreement, offer definitive answers that must be taken into consideration. Archaeology gives us a contextual approach to understanding ancient texts, regardless of where or when such texts originated.

The Bible is the source of values, legends, memories, and traditions; it is the narrative of Western civilization. It is the foundation on which Christianity and Islamic theology stand, as well as one of the binding factors that holds the Jewish people together. It is made up of the Torah or Pentateuch (literally "Five Books" in Greek), the books of the Prophets, and the Writings. The Torah is composed of Genesis, Exodus, Leviticus, Numbers, and Deuteronomy; its narrative spans the Creation, the Flood and the time of the Patriarchs, and moves on to the Exodus from Egypt, the wandering in the desert and the Revelation at Mount Sinai, concluding with the death of Moses, and the Israelite entry into Canaan. The Biblical books associated with the Prophets are generally divided into two units: the books of the Early Prophets tell the stories of Joshua, Judges I and II, Samuel I and II, and Kings I and II. These books recall the entry from Jordan and the conquest of Canaan through the rise of the Israelite Kingdom, its division and the exile of the Northern Kingdom at the hands of the Assyrians, as well as the Babylonian Exile. The Later Prophets cover a period of approximately 250 years, from the mid-8th

1

century BCE to the end of the 5th century BCE. The third section, sometimes known as the Writings, was recorded from the 5th to the 2nd century BCE; since the Writings follows the interface of modern archaeology and the Biblical narrative, it will be discussed here only briefly.

Despite all the investigation into its origin, the Bible remains a mystery that goes beyond the archaeological record. However, its origin should not be as important as its meaning for us in the 21st century. "Would that they forsake Me, but let them keep the Torah," says Lamentations Rabbah, one of the oldest works of Talmudic literature. The memories woven into the Torah narrative reflect how religion works in the mind of the reader. Y. H. Yerushalmi, professor of Jewish history, culture and society at Columbia University, tells us not to confuse memory with history. The essence of our history is not merely a question of whether all of this really happened but rather one of what these events convey to us over a period of approximately 2,200 years.

Increased awareness of the importance of material finds has demanded a reassessment of the older sources, resulting in a new acceptance of the archaeological finds. We have to face candidly the hard questions that have perplexed scholars about the reconciliation of the Biblical narrative that has come down to us with the evidence that has come up from archaeological excavation. The dust is settling and the epic of the Bible is becoming clearer. Let's look through the eyes of the archaeologist and see what history has given us to explain the actual events that occurred from the 16th century through the 6th century BCE.

Archaeology is the study of ancient artifacts of various materials in order to explain previous cultures and societies. Unlike mathematics, archaeology is not a perfect science, since archaeological finds are subject to interpretation, which in the past has often been biased by personal prejudice, politics, or economic status. Today, however, archaeological evidence is rigorously tested by scientific methods, and much attention is given to results by the professional archaeological community. Comparative analysis correctly places the material finds in their proper context so that there is little or no room for irrational hypothesis or unfounded concepts. More than 150 years of excavation have refined the methodology of this discipline. Historians usually demand that archaeologists produce outside sources to corroborate excavation findings, while archaeologists continue to excavate, interpreting their work in ways not always dependent on historical input.

The earliest archaeological excavations began in Italy more than 250 years ago at Herculaneum (1738) and Pompeii (1748). In the 1870s Heinrich Schliemann's fascination with Homer's Iliad and Odyssey led to the discovery of Troy in western Turkey. Schliemann left his mark on early archaeology by using a scientific approach to excavation. The first archaeologists were explorers, often looking for the lost wonders of the ancient world, and generally supported financially by public subscriptions or their own funds. Many expeditions were financed by universities and libraries in the major cities of France, England, Italy, and Germany, and their reports along with the retrieved objects are still in the vaults of those institutions.

During the following 150 years, several explorers, scholars, clergy, and treasure-hunters traveled from Europe to the Middle East where they found disease and hostile locals more readily than they were able to unearth buried "treasure." At the end of the 18th century CE, Napoleon Bonaparte assembled a team of scholars and scientists to survey Egypt. Their work led to the discovery of the Rosetta Stone, which offered the key to deciphering Egyptian hieroglyphics.

Another exacting basis for questioning the Biblical narrative took shape in 1830 when Charles Lyell published *Principles of Geology* which described the Geologic Column, setting the stage for Charles Darwin's *On the Origin of Species* in 1859. Darwin's theories on evolution led to an increase in Biblically-based approaches to exploration in the Fertile Crescent.

The Palestine Exploration Fund (PEF) was established in London, England, in 1865. The Fund's support of the field of Biblical Archaeology led to the creation of some of the earliest and most important surveys and maps of early Jerusalem. The PEF was also one of the first organizations to use a scientific approach to archaeology. It sponsored the work of Sir William Mathew Flinders Petrie (1853-1942), who introduced the practice of systematic and controlled archaeological excavation. Flinders Petrie first defined the method of ceramic typology, in which he compared the pottery of Egypt and Mesopotamia in several periods and saw a systematic development in decoration and manufacture of ordinary table and cookware. This helped to steer the direction of Biblical studies into a more scientific realm.

The PEF sponsored Flinders Petrie at Tel-el-Hesi, but he returned to Egypt after a year and his work was continued by F. J. Bliss (1857-1939), whose work was later condemned due to his arbitrary trench excavation and lack of methodology. It was only after Bliss teamed up with R.A.S. Macalister in a regional archaeological project in the Shephelah region that he produced a chronological sequence of artifacts from the Bronze Age to the time of the Crusades.

Macalister's work at Gezer was also questionable. He discovered only eight strata (horizontal layers of material), although in the 1970s W. G. Dever returned to the site and was able to identify 26 strata. Describing Macalister's publication on Gezer, Dever referred to the report as a vast treasure house of intriguing but often useless information (Dever 1980, p. 42).

This was followed by W. F. Albright (1891-1971), regarded as the father of Biblical Archaeology, who produced more than 1,000 publications that emphasized the relationship between Biblical authentication and the field of archaeology. This was in reaction to Biblical criticism, particularly the school of Julius Wellhausen, which proclaimed that the Biblical narrative contained little or no information of true historical value. Albright's work was also questioned by later archaeologists and many of his theories have become passé, although he is still considered to be the founder of "serious" Biblical Archaeology. The opening of the W. F. Albright Institute of Archaeological Research in Jerusalem generated a new wave of American interest in Syro-Palestinean archaeology. George Andrew Reisner (1867-1942) led the first American excavation carried out in association with Harvard University without so-called "biblical baggage" (Silberman, 1982).

One of Albright's students, Nelson Glueck (1900-1971), was said to have excavated with a spade in one hand and a Bible in the other. He was espe-cially interested in the study of settlement patterns and archaeological survey in Israel and Transjordan. In the late 1930s Glueck undertook the search for evidence of King Solomon under the aegis of Hebrew University. Excavating Tel-el-Khaleifeh at the northern tip of the Gulf of Aqaba, Glueck identified this tel with Ezion-Geber, the port from which Solomon traded exotic goods from far-flung ports. Using unorthodox archaeological methods, Glueck produced a fantasy based on the Biblical text, not on the archaeological evi-dence. Some years later, the tel was confirmed as a sand dune. Glueck was a personality with great public appeal, especially after his picture appeared on the cover of *Time* magazine following the publication of his book *Rivers in the Desert* in 1959. Later generations of archaeologists, however, found his work biased and problematic.

G. E. Wright (1909-1974) followed in the footsteps of Albright and wrote the first pottery typology for the Levant, *The Pottery of Palestine from the Earliest Time to the End of the Bronze Age*, using techniques introduced by Dame Kathleen Kenyon. However, his bold statements about the authenticity of these ceramics were rejected decades later. Scholars who studied under Wright at Harvard include W. G. Dever and L. Stager who have become well-known archaeologists today. Scholars of the conservative school used material finds to support their interpretations which were, in turn, based on the Biblical narrative. Their excavation reports were often contrived and were later disproved by more up-to-date excavation or newer scientific methods.

Today modern archaeology encompasses a wide variety of disciplines. Its basis is the excavation of materials according to a systematic procedure, along with research and comparative studies. Petrographic analysis and mi-croscopic study of ceramic fabric, including types of clay, has become im-portant to the archaeologist. In addition to material finds, studies in zoology, geology, chemistry, geography, and botany are increasingly important in understanding the world as it was in ancient times. While field work continues to be primary, reconstruction of the past through state-of-the-art computer science, statistical studies, and more accurate dating, as well as increased knowledge of the ancient civilizations in the Eastern Mediterranean, has enabled us to better understand the daily lives of the people and reconstruct history from the time of the Bible (Figure 1.1).

Bible history is derived from myths, stories, and tales handed down over time until they have became the nucleus of the literature composed by the Biblical authors. Some of this material may have actual basis in fact and helps to preserve pre-Israelite traditions; however, personal bias could have accounted for the other stories that are now believed to be hypothetical. The format of the Biblical writing, especially from the Pentateuch, reached its final state due to the efforts of redactors who supported a historical reconstruction that had little connection to actual historical events. It seems that they imposed the events of their time onto their collective past.

Though the focus here is on the archaeological record, it would be remiss not to mention the Biblical interpretations rendered by Ibn Ezra, Spinoza, Hobbes, Thomas Jefferson, and Wellhausen. Traditional Biblical scholars are well versed in their ability to rationalize linguistic mistakes and impose their own later conceptions of logical thought. They may even contradict each other and may not be in agreement, but can always return to the text as "God-given testimony." The archaeological record as we know it today was not available to the early commentators and certainly not to the redactors of the Bible. If these findings had been known, the story line would have been dramatically different. The archaeological account is open to criticism and interpretation but it cannot be changed. What has been uncovered from the past reveals the emerging history of that past.

The primary concern in dismissing the Biblical text is that it is a rejection of divine revelation. But this is not necessarily so. It may be that dating was juggled in order to make the Patriarchs fit into a time frame that, in turn, would convince the early archaeologists, themselves, that there was a foundation to their conclusions. It was a self-fulfilling prophecy. They wanted to "save" the Bible. Most of them were steeped in the Biblical text from childhood and were looking for the truth in the ancient narrative.

By examining the Sumerian culture we can begin to appreciate the contribution of early civilizations to the development of the emerging Biblical concepts. Around 3500 BCE, it is believed that the Semitic population of southern Mesopotamia was displaced by a non-Semitic race whose principal city came to be known as Sumer. This royal city-state built its success on complex water systems and commerce, and it was here for the first time (as far as we know now) that people recorded ideas and events in writing.

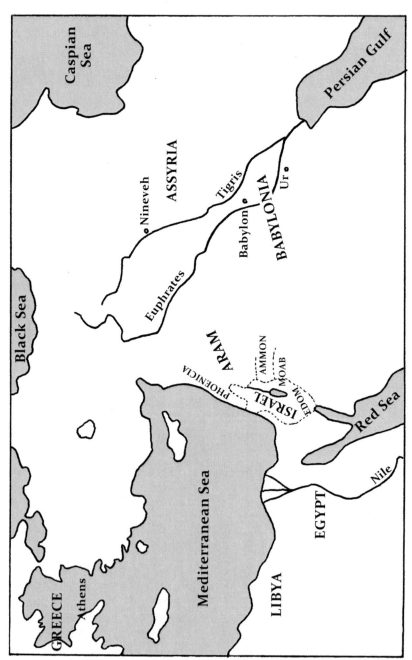

Figure 1.1.   The Eastern Mediterranean in ancient times.

They built ziggurats—artificial mountains to house sanctuaries for their gods (Figure 1.2). Hundreds of small clay tablets inscribed with pictographic signs were found in one of their temples. This was the first known writing, and later developed into what we call cuneiform. Using characters created with a wedge-shaped stylus on wet clay, the cuneiform tablets were baked and thus preserved (Figure 1.3). Over the next 1,000 years, this writing developed into sophisticated literary forms covering their theology and describing their gods, including Ashtoreth (Astarte), who is mentioned several times in the Bible.

The mythology of the Sumerians is astounding as it relates to the Biblical epic. They have the oldest recorded creation myth which parallels the story of the Flood in the Bible. The most sophisticated version is part of an epic poem about an ancient semi-legendary king, Gilgamesh, who pays a visit to the only survivor of the Great Flood. The story he is told is so close to the Biblical Flood story that the Bible account must have been directly lifted from this earlier source. In the Gilgamesh epic, the king is instructed to build a large cube-shaped vessel into which he could take "the seed of all living things." After the rains are finished, the cube settles on the top of Mount Nisir and the Sumerians send out a swallow, a raven, and a dove. Sacrifices are offered and the wording in the Gilgamesh epic is almost identical to the Biblical account: ". . . and the Lord smelled a sweet savour" (Genesis 21:21). At Megiddo, in 1955, the chance discovery of a cuneiform tablet with forty lines of the Gilgamesh epic attested to the widespread knowledge of this ancient tale. It certainly predates the Bible by several hundred years and is an indication of the spread of the Sumerian culture (Magnusson 1977, pp. 22-24).

Recently a small (2.5 cm) fragment from a cuneiform tablet was discovered in Jerusalem. The archaeologist at the south-eastern corner of the Ophel at the Temple Mount in Jerusalem stated that this fragment suggests that Jerusalem

Figure 1.2.   Ziggurat: stepped pyramid made of mud brick. Mesopotamia, 2100 BCE.

Figure 1.3. First cuneiform alphabet: thirty characters on clay tablet. Ugaritic script, approximately 2000 BCE.

must have been a large and important city in the time of Sumer, boasting significant tablets such as the one from which this piece came. This announcement was met with skepticism in the archaeological community.

Some 300 years prior to Hammurabi, the Ur-Nuzi Code was written near Babylon during the final dynasty of the Sumerian kings. The code contained approximately 60 laws dealing with inheritance, family discord, crime, rights of the underprivileged and economic settlements. Some of these were even more liberal than the laws appearing in the Code of Hammurabi. American archaeologists were involved in the excavations in Nuzi in northern Iraq between 1925 and 1933. More than 5,000 cuneiform tablets were uncovered and attributed to the Hurrians, who were destroyed by the Assyrians in approximately 1400 BCE. These tablets also dealt with daily life of the people, especially in areas concerned with arrangements of marriage, deathbed blessings, adoption, and inheritance. One of the options for a patriarch without a son was to father a child with his wife's personal slave. Another portion of the tablets deals with a Hurrian man who adopted a Hurrian woman as both his sister as well as his wife, paralleling the stories of Abraham in Genesis 12:10 and later in Genesis 20:1-16, where Sarah, the wife of Abraham, is introduced as his sister.

In 1964 Tel Mardikh, a Syrian site about 35 miles southwest of Aleppo, was excavated by Italian archaeologists working with the State Museum of Syria. Tel Mardikh housed the Ebla Tablets, an archive of about 15,000 cuneiform tables dating from 2259 BCE. The tablets are written in the Eblaite form of Sumerian script, which is considered to be the earliest Semitic language. This early Canaanite script is the direct ancestor of Hebrew and other West Semitic languages. The city was identified by a statue dedicated to the goddess Ishtar bearing the name of a king of Ebla who was known from Akkadian and Egyptian inscriptions.

One of the most enlightening of all the bodies of law from antiquity is the Code of Hammurabi (Figure 1.4). It predates the traditional Revelation at Sinai by 400 years. This eight-foot-high black basalt stele, dating from approximately 1750 BCE, gives us an insight into the life and thinking of the great Babylonian king Hammurabi. The stele was discovered by French archaeologists and resides in the Louvre. The stele lists more than 280 laws of justice and loving-kindness such as, "To cause justice to prevail in the land, to destroy wickedness and evil doing, that the weak will not be oppressed by the strong" (Code of Hammurabi). Punishments for crimes were stipulated and the concept of an "eye for an eye" was established. The care of widows was outlined, orphans were protected and incest and sexual abuses were dealt with severely (The Royal Archive of Ebla, Skira, 2007).

According to Genesis 11:31, Abraham left Ur of the Chaldeans and could have passed through the city of Mari (in modern Syria near the Iraqi border) on his way to Haran. It was on the site of Mari that André Parrot excavated the Royal Palace at Tell Hariri in 1933. Here much information about the cultural and socio-economic conditions was found inscribed on over 25,000 cuneiform clay tablets written in Akkadian (Figure 1.5). The tablets addressed issues such as the slaughtering of animals as a mark of covenant, procedures for inheritance and adoption, and the role of judges, as well as

Figure 1.4. Law Code of Hammurabi, Ur, 1750 BCE.

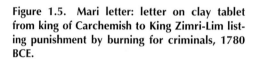

Figure 1.5. Mari letter: letter on clay tablet from king of Carchemish to King Zimri-Lim listing punishment by burning for criminals, 1780 BCE.

tablets of prophetic messages. Mari was overrun by Hammurabi's forces in approximately 1760 BCE.

Although there were many claims by the leading Italian archaeologists at the site of Mari as to the similarities in names and sites in the tablets relating to the Biblical Patriarchs, Yahweh worship, and the prophets, it is now accepted that "Ebla has no bearing on these subjects and is studied above all as an incipient civilization in its own right" (Chavalas and Younger 2002, p. 41). However Ebla does describe names that have been handed down and must have been in use throughout the area. Professor Paolo Mattinc of the University of Rome led the excavations under the slopes of the city's acropolis in 1973, when a large building previously thought to be the royal palace library actually turned out to be the archive of the quartermaster. The excavators realized that Middle Bronze Age Ebla had been destroyed in 1600 BCE, and was actually built on an earlier city that had been destroyed by fire around 2250 BCE. They discovered 42 more inscribed tablets dealing with commercial or administrative matters in what was apparently the repository of the official state archives of Ebla between 2400 and 2250 BCE.

Dr. J. H. Hertz, late Chief Rabbi of the British Empire, discusses the relationship between Moses and the Hammurabi Code. "It is now admitted that some of the stories of the Patriarchs can only be fully understood in the light of the Hammurabi family and shepherd law . . . there are however twenty-four instances of analogies and resemblances between the two Codes—in regards to the laws of kidnapping, burglary, deposit, assault and various others, especially in *lex talionis*, life for life, tooth for tooth, eye for eye. Now, it is argued, in view of the fact that the Mosaic law is at least 400 years the younger of the two, these resemblances constitute strong evidence that the Hammurabi Code is the immediate or the remote source of the Mosaic civil and criminal legislation" (Hertz 1979, p. 404).

The thrust of this work is not Biblical criticism or the analysis of ancient or modern versions of the Biblical text. We are interested in bringing forward the archaeological findings of approximately the last 50 years and seeing how, if, and when they can be connected with the Biblical narrative. Biblical scholars often have their own bias or personal belief or non-beliefs which we do not want to confuse with the archaeological material evidence. This pertains to Jewish, Christian, humanistic, and atheistic scholars. Christian scholars who are looking for parallels to support their belief in Jesus as he is described in the Gospels of the New Testament, or earlier in Psalms of David or in prophets such as Isaiah, will not find these interfaces in the archaeological record. However, they will find a great deal of archaeological confirmation in the first millennium CE. In the early days of translating the Dead Sea scrolls, it was Christian scholars who played a significant role. Their findings were meager and disappointing, due to their slow and limited publication. The scrolls are comprised of over 800 documents and tens of thousands of fragments written in Hebrew, Aramaic, and Greek. Since Islam postdates the Dead Sea scrolls by 300 to 700 years, no prophetic message relates to their religion.

A word about Jerusalem and its special place in all three religions: for Jews and Muslims, Jerusalem is where the Akedah, the binding of Isaac or Ishmael, took place. Its centrality is further connected as the capital of the kingdoms of David and Solomon, the site of the Temple, the site of the Crucifixion of Jesus, and the destination of Mohammed's midnight ride as well as the city that Jews ruled in early times and again today. In Christianity, Jerusalem is more allegorical. The name has come to refer to the Church on earth and the concept of Jerusalem "on high," in the heavenly realm. These concepts are not critical to archaeological interpretation and will not be addressed in this text.

Chapter Two

The Patriarchal Period

The patriarchal period in the Bible (1900–1750 BCE), placed chronologically in the archaeological time table, cannot be accounted for historically, since it is assumed that the Israelites remained in Egypt for over 400 years. Separating the Biblical text from folklore, with the support of carefully excavated material finds, allows us to define the time frame in which Israelite history took place. Using archaeological evidence, it is possible to understand the events concerning the Patriarchs in the Biblical book of Genesis.

Canaan, the physical setting for the period of the Patriarchs, has long been characterized as a land bridge between Asia and Africa. The armies of Mesopotamia in the north and Egypt in the south were constantly trying to defeat each other. Thus by the beginning of the second millennium BCE the area's natural resources and indigenous culture was destroyed. With all the trauma of wars and population shifts, this sliver of land with its Canaanite inhabitants and Semitic tribes was continually influenced by the Mesopotamian and Egyptian cultures. Throughout this period, the petty kings of Canaan could not create a coalition, and continually fought against each other to gain control of the surrounding territories.

Archaeologists excavating in early Bronze Age (3100-1850 BCE) sites in Iraq have uncovered material in the Mari texts and second millennia texts from Nuzi, which suggest that many of the accounts in Genesis were influenced by earlier writings. It is the mythology of the Sumerians which is most germane to the exploration of the patriarchal saga. They recorded the oldest known myths—stories about Creation that became the basis of several parts of the book of Genesis transcribed many centuries later.

In the story of Cain and Abel, Cain's Hebrew name is also the name of the tribe of the Kenites, a people who were part of the Midianite culture. These people probably settled on the border of Judah in the 10th century BCE and were incorporated into the tribe of Judah. Jethro, father-in-law of Moses, is said to have been a Kenite (Judges 1:16). This and the earlier stories in Genesis are etiological tales. That is, they are created to convey an ethical or political message. Names from the patriarchal age such as Ab-ra-mo (Abraham), E-sa-um (Esau), and Ish-ma-ilu (Ishmael) are personal names, mentioned in the Bible.

These names also appear in the Ebla Texts, discovered in Syria and recognized as a major source of information about the Sumerian empire. King Beer, the third and most powerful of the six kings of the Ebla dynasty (2400-2250 BCE), had the same name as Eber, one of the descendents of the Israelites (Genesis 10:24 and 11: 15). These legends were told not as history or literature, but rather to present a situation that was happening at that time, which could be conveyed easily, had interesting content, and later could be transcribed by a scribe. They were usually based on a previous tale that had been handed down orally through the generations.

Once the Biblical narrative gets past the engaging and mythological aspects such as Creation and Noah's Ark, the name of Abraham becomes the driving force. Abraham is portrayed as the progenitor of the age of the Patriarchs and the ancestor of the children of Israel. The disputed date of this period varies from 2000 to 1700 BCE; there is no historical reference other than the Bible itself, which does not deal in actual time. This time frame has to be re-examined again, as it has already been radically revised by Biblical scholars as well as archaeologists.

Patriarchal history, as described in Genesis, is an attempt to trace the genealogy from generation to generation. This transmission can be seen in the Covenant between God and Abraham: "To your offspring I assign this land from the river in Egypt to the great river of the Euphrates" (Genesis 14:18). The boundaries given, which include Tyre, Sidon, Lebanon, and Byblos, represent a generalized ideal. The Patriarchs (Abraham, his son Isaac, and Isaac's son Jacob) are the founders of ancient Israel. Jacob, also known as Israel, had 12 sons who are designated as the 12 tribes of Israel. According to Genesis 11:31, Abram (later Abraham) took his family from Ur of the Chaldees to the land of Canaan.

The archaeological record tells us, however that Ur of the Chaldees did not exist until approximately 800 years after the time of Abraham. The city of Ur predated the Chaldeans and thrived as one of the largest cities of its time (2500 BCE). It is mentioned four times in the Bible with the Hebrew word "Kesdim" rendered as "Chaldeans" (Genesis 11:28, 11:31, and 15:7; and Nehemiah 9:7). The redactors used "Ur of the Chaldees" since it was the political reality of the time in which they were writing. Their use of the expression "of the Chaldees" tells us that the Chaldeans had already captured the throne of Babylon and ruled the entire region (8th to 7th century BCE). Babylon is known as Tel Maqayyar in modern Iraq, where the British Museum began excavating in 1919, followed by the University of Pennsylvania. The Ziggurat, the Shrine of the Temple area, and the Royal Cemetery were among the many treasures uncovered.

This is only one of many instances in the Pentateuch of the misplacement of sequences of historical events that occurred almost one thousand years later, according to written documents. Another example is found in Genesis 36:31: "These are the kings who reigned in the land of Edom before any king reigned over the Israelites." This passage assumes the knowledge that kings eventually ruled over Israel, an event that did not happen until the time of Saul and David, several hundred years later.

The actual individuals mentioned in the Bible probably did not exist. Their personalities described in the text may bear similarities to characters, lifestyles, and cultures of the times. There are no historical parallels or archaeological patterns to support the great Biblical family saga that begins with Abraham, chosen by God to lead his people from Mesopotamia to the land of Canaan and build a great nation. The travels and experiences Abraham encountered with his family as they wandered in foreign environments, entered the new homeland, and fled to Egypt are all enduring and engaging stories, reflecting the history of the late 10th to 8th century BCE, but projected back onto the characters of the patriarchal period. Several names and places used in the contents of the early time periods did not exist until the 10th to 8th centuries. The Arameans, represented as the ancestors of Abraham, are not mentioned as a group prior to the 11th century BCE and only became an important tribe on the borders of Israel in the 9th century BCE.

In Genesis, the entire story of Abraham's family lineage is compressed, starting with Noah and the Flood and proceeding to his sons Shem, Ham, Japeth, and their progeny. There are long lists of who begat whom until Abraham, who leaves Ur of the Chaldees with his wife, his kinsmen and his flocks. If taken literally, this history would have spanned several centuries.

Today if one observes Bedouin life in the Levant, it is easy to draw parallels with ancient customs and even with the extended journey of Abraham from Ur to Canaan. It is understandable then that the patriarchal narrative was widely accepted as the typical pastoral lifestyle of the early Bronze Age. Even the father of Biblical archaeology, William F. Albright, repeated this hypothesis.

Using the 15th century BCE Nuzi archive excavated in Northern Iraq, archaeologists juggled the dates set by their earlier colleagues in order to make the patriarchal period fit a time frame that would be more convincing to Biblical scholars. An example of this maneuvering is the repeated mention of camels in the Biblical account. In Genesis 37:25, camels are described as beasts of burden, used in caravans, as in the Joseph story. However, camels were not domesticated for caravan use until Iron Age II (1000-580 BCE), and the merchandise mentioned (gum, balm, and myrrh) was most widely traded in the 8th century BCE during the Assyrian period. An assemblage of camel bones excavated at Tell Jemmah near Gaza in Israel, on the main caravan route, shows a dramatic increase in the number of mature camels in the 7th century. This could indicate that the flock was not raised locally, and could have been the bones of camels who died en route (Wapnish 1981, pp. 101-102; Finkelstein and Silberman 2002, pp. 3 and 267).

The period of unrest in Egypt began, according to Exodus 1:8, when a new king came to power. Several years had passed since Joseph had been the grand vizier and the new ruler "did not know Joseph." It is now clear that these new kings were of Asiatic descent, interlopers from Canaan, who ruled in the Nile Delta during the 15th dynasty (1500-640 BCE). The excavations at Tell el-Dab'a, considered to be Avaris, the Hyksos capital, yielded material finds suggesting that the Hyksos were Canaanite in origin. Three of the six names that appear on the ancient Egyptian kings list are clearly Semitic. One of them is the Amorite/Canaanite name Yaqub, the equivalent of the Hebrew name of the Biblical Patriarch Jacob. It is very possible that the Exodus, recorded 900 years later, was a remnant of these earlier folktales. It appears that the Joseph saga as well, with its dramatic narrative, may be a separate story that was later incorporated into the larger saga. Joseph, the youngest son of Jacob the Patriarch and his wife Rachel, was sold into slavery by his brothers, rescued by the Midianites, and sold again to the Egyptians. Ultimately, using his wits, Joseph became the viceroy of Egypt and is finally reconciled with his brothers and his father. This is folklore in its own right.

The Cave of Machpelah in Hebron (Genesis 23), where Abraham is said to have buried his wife, Sarah, eventually became known as the burial site of the three patriarchal figures, Abraham, Isaac, and Jacob (Figure 2.1). Three of their four wives (Sarah, Rebekah, and Leah) are also said to have been interred there. (Rachel, Jacob's second wife, is buried on the way to Bethlehem.) On examination, it is evident that this "cave" is in fact a manmade water cistern. Below the cenotaph (empty tomb) marking the spot known as the Tombs of the Patriarchs are Crusader burial chambers. King Herod (who ruled Israel from 37-4 BCE) built a large structure here to show the Judeans that he was a committed believer, although he was a descendent of a forced convert and was never accepted by the priestly class or the people. With the advent of Islam in 632 CE, the mihrab (prayer niche facing toward Mecca) was added to the main hall to acknowledge the new religion's veneration of the Patriarchs.

Figure 2.1. Cave of Machpelah, with later construction by Herod, 1st century BCE.

The search for the historical Patriarchs has continued to the present time with great zest. Most of the historical periods of the Patriarchs suggested by the Bible parallel the archaeological record. Circular argumentation in which the Biblical text serves as primary evidence of its own historical proof is frequently cited as evidence. Since no written records other than the Bible remain, it is only through analytical research and deduction that the historical periods and lost cultures can be reconstructed (Finkelstein and Mazar 2008, p. 28). Further, the absence of evidence is not evidence of absence and does not apply in the patriarchal period. Most scholars have now abandoned the picture of the Biblical text for the patriarchal period and settlement in the land (Grabbe 2007, p. 23).

It is generally accepted that the patriarchal stories were transmitted orally, more or less unchanged by the indigenous cultures in Canaan during the 12th and 11th centuries BCE, until they were written down as late as the 7th and 6th centuries BCE. Events in the 8th century BCE created the need to construct and articulate a comprehensive historical past, a perspective of history which would give meaningful context to the identity of the Hebrews and to the special relationship they felt with their God. The Assyrian conquest of the Northern Kingdom of Israel in 722 BCE led to the Babylonian Exile, which caused many of the inhabitants of the north to flee to Judea in the south, while many others were taken into captivity or exiled.

The archaeological record was not available to the early commentators and certainly not to the earliest scribes of the Bible. If it had been, the story line would have been dramatically different. The archaeological account, while it cannot be changed, can be criticized and is open to discussion. What was uncovered in excavation reveals the actual history of the past. The narrative of the patriarchal tradition is the folk tale motif assigned to these personalities in a sit-com form and adapted in order to convey a moral and theological framework.

The transmission of these narratives, with their cultural memories and folkloric stories handed down through the ages, is what constitutes tradition. Professor Michael Fishbane, the Nathan Cummings Professor of Jewish Studies at the University of Chicago, best describes this process: "Tradition assumes religious dignity through its exegetical associations with revealed scripture." Professor Fishbane describes two distinct types of exegetical tradition: one dignified by its verbal origins in scripture, and the other dignified by the religious community which lives by that scripture and whose customs, therefore, can be faithfully regarded as a form of non-verbal exegesis. "Scribes received the texts of tradition, studied and copied them, puzzled about their contents and preserved their meanings for new generations. Whatever the origin and history of our Biblical materials, they then became manuscripts in the hands of scribes, and it is, as such, that we have received them. The transmission of these stories-folklore-traditions was probably carried out by a class of Jewish scribes which emerged in the post exilic period and are referred to in Scriptures and in Rabbinical literature, which had a major part in the momentous events and transformation of ancient Israel into ancient Judaism and ancient Israelite exegesis into ancient Jewish exegesis" (Fishbane 1985, pp. 23-24).

The technical title of "scribe" first appeared in the royal council established by King David at the outset of the United Monarchy (II Samuel 8:16-17) and in the Torah in the book of Deuteronomy. This office appears to have remained a component of the royal bureaucracy for at least 300 years from the beginning of the 10th century to the 7th century BCE (Fishbane 1985, p. 25). This scribal tradition may be the link between the oral and written transmission of the Bible. Scribes were not necessarily priests. The Jerusalem priesthood was descended from Aaron. At Bethel King Jeroboam appointed priests. In the north, Levites functioned as priests in Shiloh and there were rural Levites who functioned at various high places for most of the history of Israel and Judah. There were also Mushite priests, who considered themselves descendents of Moses (Friedman 1989, p. 120). It was Hezekiah in II Chronicles 32:2 who formalized the divisions of the priests and the Levites.

Though it appears that the Patriarchs did not exist as described in the Biblical narrative, they are not absent! They live in the social enterprise of the Biblical world and continue to have a central place in theological thought. They are an ever-present expression of belief, which cannot be dismissed as folklore. Their early teachings have been internalized into a complex set of living traditions which have been absorbed by Judaism, Christianity, and Islam.

Chapter Three

The Exodus

Leaving Egypt and Wandering in the Desert

The Exodus, the period of wandering in the desert, the Burning Bush, the Revelation at Sinai . . . these are the touchstones of the Israelite experience according to the Biblical narrative. They are a major part of the foundation upon which Judeo-Christian tradition is based, but the historical credibility of the Biblical description does not match the archaeological chronology or material finds from the Late Bronze period (1550-1200 BCE).

According to the Bible, the families that followed Joseph to Egypt spent 430 years there and multiplied miraculously (Exodus 12:40). This ought to make it reasonable to fit the Israelite presence in Egypt into an identifiable historical context. Egypt's history is well documented and the Biblical account is quite explicit in its detail. An exodus of such epic proportion, made up of 603,550 men under the age of 20 along with women, children, and support groups, could not have been overlooked, although it was customary in Egypt to obliterate evidence of any defeats or negative circumstances. This can be seen in the destruction of monumental buildings, the erasure of documents, and the changing of doubtful outcomes to positive conclusions. Despite the large number of contemporary records uncovered, there is not one historical reference to the presence of the Israelites in Egypt at this time. There is no mention of Joseph, who acted as the pharaoh's grand vizier, nor any word about Moses, the massive Exodus of his followers, or the disappearance of the pursuing Egyptians into the Red Sea. According to the traditional timeframe, the Exodus is dated to approximately 1300 BCE. This would be when the Hebrew slaves left Egypt and headed toward the Sinai Desert.

Many far-fetched explanations exist for the occurrence of the plagues that forced the pharaoh to let the Israelites go. Some of the explanations are based on natural phenomena, while others fall into the realm of miracles. The adventure-seekers who pursue such paths are trying to rationalize these occurrences, while those who want to believe in miracles accept what is written. If one has faith in these miracles, no rational person or explanation is likely to dissuade them. Faith is based on feelings, not facts, and feelings are not right or wrong . . . they just are! They belong to the believer and are rooted in his consciousness.

Dr. S. H. Parcak serves as an assistant professor in the department of anthropology at the University of Alabama. She has employed a combination of satellite-image analysis and surface surveys that have allowed her to isolate water sources in the Sinai Desert. Using satellite imaging technology, her work has enabled archaeologists to examine a broad spectrum of archaeological sites both on and beneath the surface; the surveys also reveal any remains of buildings or destruction below the present ground level. No water sources large enough to support the vast number of people described in the Biblical epic have come to light anywhere along the route of the Exodus as it is described in the Bible.

The source of the Nile rises in modern-day Uganda, in the Central African highlands. That same Nile River winds its way northward to become the heart of Egypt's agricultural existence, as well as the main source of water for the Egyptian population. In times of famine or drought, the river has served as a reservoir for lands as far away as Canaan, where people depended on the Nile's seasonal rainfall. Two maps from the Roman Byzantine period show the Nile with seven branches in the delta, a much wider area of water than the two branches that exist today. The present constellation of the river is the result of a build up of sediment. In Biblical times it is likely that farmers and semi-nomadic people settled in the area of the delta.

The land of Goshen lies in the northeastern area of Egypt. It is the name applied to the area where Jacob and his extended family of pastoralists settled. It is also called the land of Ramesses, described as being separate from Egypt, and good for livestock and crops. The area is also identified as the 20th name of Egypt in the eastern delta, as well as being known as Gesem during the Twenty-sixth dynasty in Egypt (672-525 BCE). This area encompasses the western end of Wadi Tumilat on the eastern border close to the city of Succoth. Pithom was a main city, which extended to the north abutting the land of Ramesses. The dating of the Twenty-sixth dynasty interfaces with the accepted time that the settlement in Goshen was amended into the Bible text by scribes at the end of the 7th century BCE.

Archaeologists have long sought evidence of the Egyptian role in the Biblical account surrounding Joseph, Moses, and the Exodus. Egyptian inscriptions and depictions indicate that Asiatics from Canaan and surrounding lands in West Asia entered Egypt as traders, migrants, or captives during the second millennium BCE. No proof has surfaced that the Hebrews lived in Egypt at that time. Most historians and archaeologists doubt that an entire group of people with distinct customs and beliefs could have entered Egypt, been enslaved, and then escaped en masse without leaving a trace, as depicted in the Biblical narrative (Redford 1979, pp. 38-47).

In the eastern Nile Delta, approximately 200 miles east of Cairo, the Beni Hassan tomb paintings from the 19th century BCE show Asiatic people immigrating to Egypt. This is often cited as the most celebrated evidence of the journey of Abraham, and later Jacob, to Egypt. It depicts 37 Semites along with laden donkeys entering Egypt, escorted by frontier officials. This painting has been repeatedly identified as an authentic picture of the arrival in Egypt of a Semitic family, similar to Abraham and Jacob's entry into Egypt in time of famine. Beni Hassan has become the model for our idealization of these events. However, the accompanying text found in the excavation, written in Egyptian hieroglyphics, makes it clear that the people shown are traders, bringing a cargo of lead sulphide from the area of the Red Sea. This chemical was used for eye cosmetics and medical purposes in the ancient world.

Egypt was ruled by the Hyksos during the Middle Bronze period, as evidenced by inscriptions and seals with names of Hyksos rulers that were found in Canaan. Many major Hyksos cities were located in the eastern delta, including Tell el-Yehudiyah, Heliopolis, Tell el-Maskhuta, and Tell el-Dab'a. Of these, Tell el-Dab'a, considered to be Avaris, the ancient Hyksos capital, represents the best example of an Asiatic presence. It was here that the Hyksos kings installed a garrison of no less than 240,000 troops according to Manetho, an Egyptian historian of the 3rd century BCE, long after the Hyksos were expelled from Egypt. Anthropologists have identified 134 bodies from Hyksos-period cemeteries at Tel el-Dab'a. These remains are more consistent with north and central European origins rather than the West Semitic populations that might have been expected in Canaan at the time.

Fundamentalists try to slot the Joseph episode into the Hyksos period. In a monograph, "A Study of the Biblical Story of Joseph," Egyptologist and archaeologist Donald Redford, professor of classical and ancient Mediterranean studies at Pennsylvania State University, states that the Egyptian elements and plot motifs in the story do not reflect the 17th century BCE but rather the 7th century BCE at the earliest. Redford infers that the geographic and socio-economic details of the Exodus epic are based on prevailing conditions in Judah during the 7th century BCE. The Joseph story has no independent historical validity and is a relocation of another bondage—namely, the Babylonian Exile in the 6th century BCE which was imminent at the time the Bible account was written down. This could have provided 6th-century scribes with a chance to shape the tradition into its present epic form, as it offered exiles the knowledge that they would eventually be delivered, just as their ancestors had been freed from bondage in Egypt.

Excavations on the eastern side of the Nile Delta suggest a Canaanite takeover of power and continued Canaanite presence in the delta until their expulsion around 1570 BCE. Once again, this time frame does not match the Biblical narrative. The city of Ramesses was built by Pharaoh Ramesses II who ruled from 1279-1213 BCE. The idea that Semitic slaves were used in the construction of this city presents a conflict in dating. The Pharaoh Merneptah, son of Ramesses II, mentions Israel on his victory stele, which dates from 1208 BCE. According to the Biblical narrative, this would be after the Exodus, the period of wandering in the desert, and the death of Moses. No mention of Israel has been found in any of the inscriptions and documents connected with the Hyksos period. Nor is Israel mentioned in the 14th century BCE cuneiform archive found at Tell el-Amarna in Egypt, where more than 400 letters describe in detail the social, political, and demographic situation in Canaan at that time (Figure 3.1). "There is no recognizable archaeological evidence of Israel's presence in Egypt immediately before that time" (Finkelstein and Silberman 2002, p. 567). Therefore, the Israelites did not build Pithom or Ramesses.

Figure 3.1. El Amarna letter: cuneiform, from vassal king in Canaan to pharaoh, 14th century BCE.

Early in the Biblical account of the wandering in the Sinai, several locations are mentioned (Figure 3.2). Only Kadesh-Barnea and Ezion-Geber can be identified today. The Israelite encampment was said to be at Kadesh-Barnea for 38 years (Numbers, chapters 13, 14, and 20). Today this is the site of Ein el-Qudeirat in the eastern Sinai. Repeated excavations, aerial photographs, and archaeological survey have shown no sign of habitation in the periods associated with the Biblical Exodus. In fact there is no archaeological evidence of occupation at Kadesh-Barnea before the 10th century BCE. There was not so much as a potsherd from the 13th to 12th centuries BCE, the time set for the Exodus (Dever 2003, p. 20). There is also evidence that the author of the Biblical narrative has drawn on topographical knowledge dating from the 8th and 7th centuries BCE to construct the route of the journey. Only at the end of Iron Age II were most of the identifiable sites actually occupied (Grabbe 2007, p. 87).

The Biblical journey proceeds across the Negev and places the wanderers in Edom, in southern Transjordan. Until approximately the 7th century BCE this area was desolate, without any tribal identity. Looking back on the Biblical account, there could not have been a king of Edom who denied access to the Israelites (Numbers 20:20-21) as no king, or kingdom, existed. This is a clear case of the scribes who wrote the book of Numbers during the 8th and 7th centuries BCE inserting a scenario of their own time into the Bible story, indicating that Edom was a problematic state at the time of writing.

Continuing in the book of Numbers, the journey shifts to Arad in the northern Negev. In 1964 Yohanan Aharoni excavated Tel Arad, approximately fifteen miles from Be'er Sheva. He found a small isolated village from the 10th century BCE that had been abandoned for 1700 years. Therefore Numbers 21:1, which states that the Israelites laid waste to Arad and destroyed all other cities in the area, could not have happened at the time of the Exodus. There is no archaeological evidence of any Bronze or Early Iron Age cities in the northern Negev, where Arad is located. This is a continuing pattern in the stories of the wandering of the Israelites. The tales of Heshbon, the Moabite campaign, Dibon, and the incursions into Midian all reflect periods of settlement 400 to 500 years after the supposed date of the Exodus. The incident of the five kings and their cities in Numbers is therefore entirely undocumented (Dever 2003, p. 35).

Ezion-Geber was excavated in 1938-1940. The site revealed Late Iron Age (7th to 8th century BCE) occupational remains, but no Late Bronze artifacts. Despite all attempts to locate the places where the Israelites camped in the Sinai, and the location of Mount Sinai itself, no evidence has been found to match the Biblical account. One must assume that the Exodus and the wandering in the desert included only a few families and the tales that have come

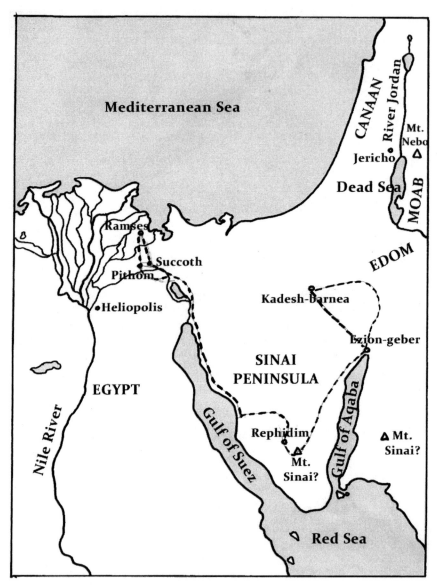

Figure 3.2.   Presumed route of the Exodus.

down to us have been inflated to fit the needs of an emerging theological ideology and incorporated into the Israelite tradition.

Egypt was the most powerful country in the Eastern Mediterranean in the 13th century BCE. Forts and strongholds were constructed from the delta to the borders of Canaan. Eliezer Oren of Ben Gurion University surveyed these fortresses in the 1970s. Any large group of people would certainly have been challenged by the military might of Egypt. The Bible tells us that more than 600,000 men of military age (Numbers 33:1) left Egypt in the Exodus, which could have swelled to three or four million people when including women, children and elderly (Grabbe 2007, p. 85). It would be impossible for even a small percentage of that number to have escaped the long arm of the Egyptians, according to the archaeological record. It is inconceivable that a group of that size could have survived in the wilderness for 40 years. Despite the arguments of some fundamentalists, there is no way to salvage the Biblical text as a description of a historical event (Grabbe 2007, p. 88).

The Biblical narrative in the book of Exodus introduces a man with the Egyptian name of Moses, a common suffix in Egyptian names. Other names such as Tuthmoses (Son of Toth) or Ramesses (son of Ra) bear out this custom. The story of Moses echoes almost word for word the birth legend of King Sargon (2270-2215 BCE), who ruled the dynasty of Akkad that was founded 1000 years earlier. The legend of Sargon, as translated from ancient Near Eastern texts, reads: "My changeling mother conceived me, in secret she bore me. She set me in a basket of rushes, with bitumen, she sealed the lid. She cast me into the river which rose not over me . . . Akki, the drawer of water, took me as his son and reared me." A neo-Syrian text from the 7th century BCE, purporting to be Sargon's autobiography, relates this legend 500 years after the Biblical date of Moses.

Moses plays such a fundamental role as the founder of Israel's faith that it is almost inconceivable to think that the powerful Biblical depiction of him does not actually portray a charismatic person. On the other hand, it has been said that "Moses may not have existed, but he must have had a cousin called Moses."

According to the Biblical account, the pharaoh during the period of bondage was probably Ramesses II, and the pharaoh of the Exodus was Merneptah, following the succession list of Egyptian kings. In 1881, Merneptah's tomb was discovered on the west bank of the Nile at Thebes. Exodus 14:28 tells us that with the miracle of the parting of the sea, the pharaoh was drowned with his troops and their bodies were "no more." Yet we know that Merneptah's body was buried on dry land.

In Exodus 13:17, "God did not let them go by way of the Philistines." The Philistines are first mentioned in historical records that date from Ramesses

III approximately 300 years after the traditional date of the Exodus (1300 BCE). There is also a reference in the Bible saying that the Israelites were concerned about meeting enemies on the coastal route out of Egypt, but there is no mention of the Egyptian fortifications that would have existed then in the northern Sinai or in Canaan. This period parallels the Twenty-sixth Egyptian dynasty of the Pharaoh Seti (1313-1292 BCE). Seti was the father of Ramesses II, who was active in rebuilding the glories of the ancient kingdom. It was during this period that the city of Pithom, mentioned in the Biblical narrative, was built. According to the text, the Egyptian king ordered the Hebrews to build the royal cities of Pithom and Rameses (Exodus 1:11). Excavations at Tell el-Maskhuta, which is associated with Pithom, reveal a small settlement from the Middle Bronze Age that was not reoccupied until the 7th century BCE.

Finding the location of the Bible's Mount Sinai has become part of a Biblical treasure hunt. Sites as far away as Ethiopia, and more recently Mount Karkom in Israel's Negev region, have been suggested. The traditional location of Mount Sinai, in the mountainous region of southern Sinai, has been visited since the 4th to 6th centuries CE. Saint Catherine's Monastery was built there in the 6th century CE by the Byzantine emperor Justinian to commemorate the supposed site of the Burning Bush and the Revelation. Above the monastery is Jebel Musa, or the mountain of Moses in Arabic. Extensive excavation and surveys around the area have not yielded any evidence or trace of an ancient encampment from the 13th century BCE. Modern archaeological techniques would be capable of finding even meager material remains of pastoral nomads and their camp sites, if they existed.

If in fact the Patriarchs did not exist as portrayed in Exodus, and Moses did not deliver the Israelites from slavery, then Sinai and Revelation also must not have occurred as depicted in the Bible. The Ten Commandments (the Decalogue), which were inscribed on two tablets and revealed to Moses at Mount Sinai, could not have actually happened as described in two versions of that momentous event in Exodus 20:8-12 and in Deuteronomy 5:12-15. Both versions teach the same laws, except that Deuteronomy states, in observing the Sabbath Day, "Remember that you were slaves in the land of Egypt and the Lord your God brought you out from there with a mighty hand and outstretched arm." This same book of Deuteronomy was rediscovered in Judea during the reign of King Josiah (640-609 BCE), which is precisely the time of the interface between the Biblical narrative and the archaeological record, thus reframing the narrative as history. The two versions might also indicate slightly different recollections of two individual scribes in that period. In the Dead Sea scrolls, both versions are merged in the All Souls Deuteronomy scroll, which was written between 250 BCE and 68 CE and found among 400 other documents in Cave #4 at Qumran in 1957.

Revelation can be direct as well as indirect. According to the Biblical narrative, Moses received the Commandments by divine encounter just as the prophets received their messages through divine inspiration. We, in turn, receive these laws revealed in the Pentateuch daily. The fact that they were not revealed as portrayed in Exodus does not alter their status as the foundation of monotheistic religious practice. In the early 1960s one of the most brilliant and controversial thinkers of the modern age, Louis Jacobs, was slated to become the principal of Jews' College in London. However, he lost credibility with the Orthodox establishment on the publication of his book *We Have Reason to Believe*, in which he expressed the view that "in the Bible we have the Divine message conveyed to us through the activities and thoughts of human beings."

According to the Bible, the Golden Calf was made out of the precious material which the Israelites collected on their departure from Egypt. This episode is probably a reflection of the period in which much of the Northern Kingdom broke away from the religion of Jerusalem in the 8th century BCE, and cult practices were reinstituted. Immediately after the episode of the Golden Calf, the building of the Tabernacle is introduced. Six chapters of the book of Exodus (chapters 35 through 40) focus on this construction, which was so costly and elaborate that it would be difficult to reproduce even in modern times, especially under desert conditions. The importation of materials like acacia wood as well as the engineering skills required for the erection and transportation of a large structure like the Ark of the Covenant seem unrealistic. After the Tabernacle came to rest in the city of David (I Chronicles 15:1) in approximately 1000 BCE, it is not mentioned again.

There are no archaeological proofs that a structure like the Tabernacle ever existed or, for that matter, did not exist. In the late 19th and early 20th centuries, scholars looked upon the story of the Tabernacle as a literary fiction and suggested that it was a retrojection of the later Temple worship in Judah. More recently other researchers have tried to find parallels in tent sanctuaries found in Near Eastern cultures, suggesting that the Tabernacle is a borrowed motif from the ancient sanctuary of Ugarit. It may also be that the dimensions of the Biblical Tabernacle are nearly the same as the excavated temple in Arad.

In 1973, immediately after the Yom Kippur War, the writer was among the earliest visitors to the Sinai Peninsula. It was impossible to survey the area due to the ravages of the war and the possibilities of land mines. However, it was possible to observe the terrain with an eye toward archaeology. The Sinai is mainly a stone desert, not a sandy expanse with shifting dunes, as is generally found along the coast of the Red Sea. Any movement in the Sinai, even by small caravans, would have left their mark forever in the crusty surfaces. Aerial photography can identify these movements, along with imprints of temporary structures from antiquity. Nothing has shown up on any of the many surveys or photographs over nearly four decades since 1973. No trace has been found that could be linked with the Exodus account. Other sites listed in the Bible in connection with the giving of the Ten Commandments may be pointed out by guides, but most are mentioned for the benefit of tourists. "Lastly, all the major places that play a role in the story of the wandering of the Israelites were inhabited in the 7th century BCE. In some cases, they were occupied only at that time, which is the point at which the archaeological record and the Bible narrative interface" (Currie and Hyslop 2009).

This chapter began by inferring that the historical credibility of the Biblical description of the Exodus had no relation to the archaeological chronology or material finds. However, that does not negate the fact that the Bible's historical core rose from a spiritual, political, and ethical basis, and was driven by a "force" in response to the creative instincts that produced a responsible society which has endured and flourishes to this day. These core values reflect the ideology and the times of writers—scribes, priests, and redactors. This is an effort to reconstruct the history of ancient Israel on the basis of archaeological evidence, thus creating a more authentic past.

The book of Exodus closes as Moses is denied entry to the Promised Land. He is only allowed to view Israel from Mount Nebo, when he was 120 years old (Deuteronomy 34). Mount Nebo, associated with Jebel Musa, is some 20 miles southwest of Amman, Jordan. It is there that Moses is said to have expired, "but no man knoweth of his sepulcher until this day" (Deuteronomy 34:6). He remains in the consciousness of all Western religions . . . as it is said, Astarte never lived, but Moses never died.

Chapter Four

The Emergence of the Israelite People

The end of the Late Bronze Age was characterized by political instability, social upheaval, and the movement of populations throughout the Eastern Mediterranean (Canaan). This set the stage for new cultures and new kingdoms during the Iron Age, or from around 1200 BCE. Evidence from excavations and archaeological surveys suggests a process whereby the pastoral tribes already present in Canaan grew in number and began to settle down (Golden 2004).

The Conquest of Canaan as described in the Biblical books of Joshua and Judges has provoked much interest and debate within the archaeological community (Figure 4.1). The books themselves do not agree in their descriptions of the events that took place. Joshua tells of a more sweeping and devastating campaign than the one portrayed in Judges. Recent excavations show that Jericho, Ai, and almost all Canaanite cities (28 in total, plus cities of refuge) said to have been destroyed by Joshua were actually in ruins long before Iron Age I (1200 BCE), when an "Israelite presence" was first recorded in Egypt on the Merneptah Stele of 1203 BCE (Figure 4.2). Only two sites, Lachish and Hazor, have yielded some material finds and signs of destruction in the Late Bronze period (1550-1200 BCE). The great Canaanite city of Shechem would have been a prime target, yet it is not mentioned among Joshua's conquests, and only appears in Judges chapter 9 without any connection to conflict.

The archaeological record shows remains of local coarse pottery above the level of the rich 13th century BCE indigenous Canaanite material culture throughout the region. These material finds have yielded a tremendous amount of information in connection with the dramatic change that took place at the end of the 12th century BCE in the central hill country of Canaan. Conclusions from archaeological surveys indicate that there were no sudden invasions, and no massive destruction of Canaanite cities occurred at that

31

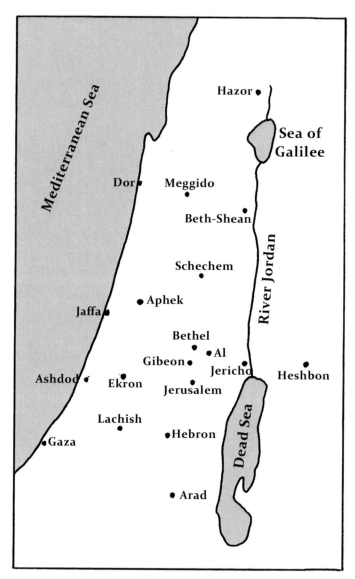

Figure 4.1.   Main sites relating to the Conquest of Canaan narrative,
11th century BCE.

Figure 4.2. Merneptah Stele, hieroglyphs on black granite, 1203 BCE.

time. Instead, there appears to have been a peaceful period of building hilltop communities, and more than 200 such sites have been recorded.

Khirbet Qeiyafa, overlooking the Elah Valley on the main road between Philistia, the Coastal Plain and the Shephelah (hill country), has been recently excavated by Professor Yosef Garfinkel and Saar Ganor. They claim the evidence found there provides proof that a unified, centralized, and politically organized Jewish kingdom existed in the time of David and Solomon. Their conclusions are based on a massive monolithic wall which required some 200,000 tons of stone. Using a small amount of olive pits found next to the wall which were carbon dated to 1051-969 BCE, the archaeologists state that the wall indicated a fortified city and is therefore an extension of the Davidic Kingdom, centered in Jerusalem. This is stretching the concept of the enlarged kingdom. The tel could have been part of the defense pattern on the border that separated the Israelites from the Philistine threat. An inscription was found in yet unknown "Hebrew script." This "news" seems to be another premature attempt to confuse Biblical events and historical fact (personally communicated to Alon Lyons by Y. Garfinkel, July 2011).

Flinders Petrie, one of the earliest archaeologists working in Egypt in the 1880s, discovered the Merneptah Stele inscribed with verses hailing the conquests of King Merneptah, who succeeded Ramesses II in 1213 BCE (Figure

4.2). The stele was installed in Thebes in the mortuary temple of Merneptah upon the king's death in 1203 BCE. This ten-foot-tall granite slab, describing the tribute that followed Merneptah's victories, was first used to commemorate an earlier king, Amenhotep III. The last two lines on the later side refer to Israel: "Plundered is Canaan with every evil, Ascalon is taken, Gezer is seized, Yenoam has become as though it never was, Israel is laid waste, its seed is not." Written in hieroglyphs, this is the earliest known reference to the people of Israel. The rest of the inscription deals mainly with a triumphant campaign that Merneptah waged against the Libyans and their allies, the Sea People, who were also called the Philistines. "The great Lord of Egypt is all powerful–victory belongs to him" (Merneptah Stele). Canaan had long been under Egyptian control, but unstable conditions made it necessary for Merneptah's forces to suppress a rebellion there. Ancient kings always made propaganda out of their victories but seldom recorded their defeats. The pictograph on the stele following the word for Israel shows a seated man and woman, indicating that the name of Israel is applied to one of the ethnic groups that lived in this area, and not to a nation or a state.

Israel Finkelstein, professor of archaeology at Tel Aviv University, has proposed that the people mentioned on the stele were pastoral shepherds who wandered throughout the Late Bronze Age in the hill area of what is today Israel. Burial remains of these people have been found without evidence of settlements, suggesting a nomadic lifestyle.

Though it was in the central region of Canaan that the kingdom of Israel would later be established, there are indications of an Israelite presence from the 12th century BCE. Canaan was under Egyptian rule during the middle of the 12th century. The presence of Egyptians is not noted in the Biblical account and was unknown to the redactors approximately 400 years later (Bietak 1979).

Intensive surveys of the earliest Israelite settlements of the early 12th to late 11th centuries BCE have been carried out since 1967 by teams of archaeologists. Advanced methodology, surface remains, and occupational evidence such as walls and pottery have all been recorded and analyzed. Estimates from surveys suggest that these communities were small, ranging in size from one to forty acres, with populations from 100 to 500 residents. At most, there were fewer than 50,000 people who can be identified with the original Israelite people. Some of these communities appear to have been settled as late as the 10th BCE and could be defined as the first Israelite settlements in Canaan. This was probably some of the most important archaeological work undertaken at that time, as it revealed a dramatic social transformation that occurred in the hill country of Canaan in approximately 1200 BCE. No remains of conflict could be identified nor was any ethnic population defined.

A revolution in lifestyle seems to have occurred. From the Judean hills in the south to the area of Samaria in the north, approximately 250 hilltop communities came to life in the 12th century BCE. These can be identified with some confidence as Israelite, since many of them were continuously occupied through the centuries up to the later period of the Monarchy. Most of the excavations in these villages showed several occupational levels, which were often renovations of the original settlement. Izbet Sartah was fully excavated by Baruch Rosen, revealing its occupation by herders and farmers. A number of innovations in technology took place in these highland communities as evidenced by terracing, plastered cisterns, Israelite four-room houses, collared rim jars, and iron tools (Dever 2003, p. 113-125).

Many of the earliest inhabitants of this area were pastoral nomads who gradually adapted to farming. It appears from animal bones collected that two different societies lived side by side. One segment consisted of traditional herders which accounted for the largest number of animal bone remains, while the other population was made up of agriculturists. It seems that the coalescence of early Israelite communities was actually a result of the collapse of the Canaanite culture, and not its cause. Most of the Israelite population emerged from indigenous people within Canaan, not from any mass exodus nor from a massive destruction or conquest, but from the local people.

The destruction carried out by the Amorite Sihon, king of the Amorites in Transjordan, after his conquests in the Negev and campaigns in the wilderness of Zin, continued in Heshbon (Numbers 21:21-32). According to the book of Numbers, Moses had sent emissaries to Sihon asking for safe passage through his territory. The king's refusal ignited a battle with the Israelites, whereupon the Israelites took possession of all of the land of Moab, including the city of Heshbon. Tel Hesban, just south of Amman, Jordan, was excavated by members of the Seventh-Day Adventist Church. They, like theologians before them, were looking forward to publishing "Biblical finds" dating from the time of the Conquest. However, only artifacts from the Iron II and III periods (1000-586 BCE) were found, dating from long after the supposed Conquest, and there were no occupation levels from the 13th to 12th century BCE. Did the Moabite campaign ever occur? Once again, we know that what was uncovered seems to fit into the context of the 7th century BCE.

Megiddo was very important, as it guarded the junction of major trade routes running from the Mediterranean coast through the hills of Samaria, across the Jezreel Valley to Lebanon and Syria. Armageddon, which is associated with Megiddo, became synonymous with apocalyptic visions of the end of the world due to the many battles that were fought there. Joshua 12 lists Megiddo as having been taken in the Conquest, while Judges 1:21 contradicts that (Dever 2003, p. 60). Megiddo has been excavated repeatedly for more than 100 years. Since 1994 the work has been under the direction of the Israel Antiquities Authority. Basically the city remained Canaanite until the late 10th century BCE with no evidence of an Israelite destruction from the 13th or 12th centuries BCE; it seems to have come under Israelite influence only during the Iron Age.

Shechem is mentioned as a major city in the Biblical narrative and was said to have been visited by Abraham (Genesis 21) and Joshua (Joshua 24). The city is not, however, mentioned in Joshua or Judges as having been conquered or destroyed at the time of the Conquest. Dever infers therefore that Shechem may have been pre-Israelite, dating back to common ancestral (patriarchal) traditions (Dever 2003, p. 62).

Gezer, another of the largest and most prominent of the Bronze and Iron Age cities, was singled out by R. A. S. Macalister for excavation in 1902. From 1964 to 1975 it was revisited under the auspices of the Hebrew Union College and the Harvard Semitic Museum, with excavations directed by W. G. Dever. This broad excavation found no Israelite destruction, despite the fact that King Merneptah on his victory stele claimed "to have captured Gezer." According to the book of Joshua (10:33) Horam, king of Gezer, joined a coalition of Canaanite kings from Lachish and other Judean sites to oppose the Israelites. "Do not drive out the Canaanites in Gezer who continue to dwell there to this day" (Joshua 16:10 and Judges 1:29). This statement seems to indicate that a long period of time had elapsed before this event finally was recorded (Figure 4.3).

Although only major excavated sites have been discussed here, W. G. Dever lists thirty-one sites mentioned in Joshua 12:9-24, of which seven are unidentified and three are unexcavated as of 1998. The rest show no dramatic Late Bronze period finds and/or no destruction levels attesting to an Israelite intrusion and conquest (Dever 2006, pp. 56-57).

Whoever the Canaanites were, they were by no means the only element in the Semitic population, which inhabited a much larger area than was previously thought. "And the territory of the Canaanites extended from Sidon in the direction of Gerar, as far as Gaza" (Genesis 10:19). The area was, in effect, a land bridge between Egypt and Mesopotamia. Excavations at Tel Mardikh suggest the existence of a great Canaanite empire in the second half of the third millennium BCE. It was frequently under the influence of Egypt in the New Kingdom period (1500-1200 BCE) and was considered an Egyptian province during this time. Politically and ethnically, it was never a homogeneous area. In the north, the Canaanites absorbed and assimilated influences from all over the known world, including Anatolia, Egypt, Mycenae, and the Aegean. From these influences, they developed a sophisticated culture and civilization.

Figure 4.3. Gezer Calendar, Phoniceo-Hebrew script on soft limestone. Record of Israelite agricultural cycle, 10th century BCE.

Since the discoveries during the excavation of Ugarit, we now have a clearer understanding of the Canaanite religious pantheon and the function and features of many of the gods. The father of the assembly of gods was El (God). He expressed the concept of ordered government and social justice. His consort was Asherah. Baal was one of the sons of El, and was a prime god of the pantheon. The chief fertility goddess was Ashtoreth; she was also associated with ritual temple prostitution. Many clay figurines of nude female figures have been found that are usually associated with the worship of Ashtoreth. It is well known that early Israelite women kept amulets with her image to insure fertility. This custom may have been the reason for the stern prohibition in the Bible against making idols (Magnusson 1977, p. 84). This example of the gradual assimilation of these people into Israelite culture can be better understood using the context of archaeological discoveries.

The sequence of finds in several Canaanite excavations shows a pattern of pastoral farming and a settled life cycle, which over time led to permanent villages. In the book of Judges, we're told that the people did not listen to their leaders and fell back to their "old ways." After wandering in the desert for 40 years, how could the Israelites have settled so quickly into communal life?

Could these have been the same Israelites mentioned in the Merneptah Stele, or the Apiru people described in the earlier Tell el-Amarna letters of the 14th century BCE? Scholars have suggested that the name Apiru has a linguistic connection to the word Ibri or Hebrew, and have inferred that the Apiru mentioned in the Egyptian correspondence were in fact the Israelites, a suggestion that has been discredited. It is now widely accepted by historians that the Apiru were bands of mercenaries and marauders with no connection to the early Israelites. They constituted a socio-economic group rather than an ethnic entity.

In the 1960s, Dame Kathleen Kenyon excavated in Jericho, the Biblical city where Joshua made his first conquest on entering the Promised Land. The results of her multi-season excavation seemed to show that Jericho was an important city of the Late Bronze-Early Iron period (around 1200 BCE). It now appears that by the time of the Conquest, Jericho was a poor, small community without defensive walls. There is no sign that a walled city existed there in the 13th century BCE. In addition, Jericho was probably abandoned for the next 500 to 600 years. It was only in the 7th to 6th century BCE, or long after the Conquest as related in the Biblical narrative, that the city was fortified once more. What Kenyon described as the Biblical fallen walls of Jericho may actually have been the dam wall of a reservoir. No destruction levels could be identified from the time of the supposed Israelite invasion.

"To many scholars, it may seem that the Deuteronomic history adapted a few stories connected specifically to the Jericho region and the territory of the Tribe of Benjamin, then used them to add detail and, thus, give an air of authenticity to its overall picture of a great Assyrian style conquest of the land" (Kugel 2007, p. 375). Rebuilt Jericho of the 7th century BCE inspired the redactors, and therefore the reconstruction is recorded in both Deuteronomy and the book of Joshua. Even the existence of a leader named Joshua is brought into question by the lack of archaeological evidence. Was he "created" by the redactors to act as the bridge between Moses and the Conquest, which may not even have taken place? In Numbers 13:16 Moses changes Joshua's given name from Hoshea to Joshua, creating a new character and personal history. Joshua, who is not mentioned in earlier episodes in the Pentateuch, thus becomes another participant in the narrative.

Further excavations in Jericho and Ai, the two cities described in detail in the book of Joshua, reaffirm that neither settlement possessed defensive walls at this time, and so were not very well fortified despite the reference to "great cities with high walls" in Deuteronomy 9:1. In fact almost all sites excavated in Canaan revealed the remains of unfortified settlements which could not qualify as cities in this period. In addition, the Biblical account is not consistent with the geopolitical reality, since Canaan was ruled by Egypt until the middle of the 12th century BCE. Administrative centers existed in Beit

She'an, Yaffo, and Gaza with Egyptian material finds. There is also no mention of Egypt in connection with the Conquest, reinforcing the understanding that the Egyptian occupation of Canaan was unknown to the redactors of the book of Joshua. These early archaeological finds reinforce the hypothesis that the redactors of the first five books of the Bible, writing in the 7th and 8th centuries BCE, were aware of the legends and social mores that existed in the past. These had been passed down through the generations and were part of the historical epic of the Israelites.

The indigenous inhabitants of Canaan may have combined with the Israelites and Asiatics from Egypt and over time melded into the Israelite people. After these "tribes" marked out their designated areas, they looked toward the surrounding lands that were not incorporated into their inheritance. Joshua lists such unincorporated areas as Gaza, Beit She'an, Megiddo, the coastal plain, and population groups who were hostile neighbors to the Israelites. The Israelites were told to evict other groups and divide the land as their inheritance (Joshua 13:1-6).

The Philistines, also known as the Sea People, were a loose confederation of several groups whose origins were in Anatolia, Crete, or other parts of the Eastern Mediterranean. They are connected by their archaeological remains, particularly their pottery, and may even be linked with the Mycenaean Greeks. They occupied Gaza, Ashkelon, Ashdod, Ekron, and Gat along Canaan's eastern plain. The Philistines are mentioned in Isaac's encounter with Avimelech, king of the Philistines, at the city of Gerar (Genesis 26:1). According to the archaeological record, the Philistines entered Canaan from the Aegean Sea as warlike invaders in the early 12th century BCE, destroying many Canaanite settlements in the process. Some Philistines became mercenaries in Egyptian garrison towns. Finds at Beit Shemesh, Ashkelon, Gezer, Beit She'an, Megiddo, and others all indicate Philistine presence, as well as those settlements on virgin soil at Tel Qasile, on the northern border of the Philistia. Tel Miqne, identified as Ekron, was the most inland city of the Philistine presence. The archaeological evidence at this site shows that the material culture was based on elements new to Canaan, which reached its peak of prosperity and political and military prowess at the end of the 11th century BCE. The development of Philistine monochrome and bichrome pottery is an important factor in dating Canaanite sites, especially in relation to cultural borders (Figure. 4.4). At Tel Miqne and Ashdod, the bichromeware is evident in the 11th and into the 10th centuries BCE (Grabbe 2002, p. 72), signifying the Philistine presence at these sites. Philistine-style pottery has been found in the northern area of Canaan as a reminder of the Philistine influence. Supposedly the tribe of Dan relocated itself to the far north as a result of the pressures of the Philistines.

Figure 4.4. Philistine bichrome-ware: typical Mycenean-style pottery found in Canaan, 11th-10th century BCE.

The Philistines were Greek speakers and generally followed the Greek culture. They were accomplished in forging metals and skilled in the use of metal arms for warfare. They wore plumed copper helmets and used chain mail, as well as shields and weapons of iron in battle. Iron was available to the Israelites, as evidenced by an iron plowshare recovered at Tell el-Ful north of Jerusalem. But bronze was more widely used until the process of tempering iron to high degree of hardness was perfected by the Philistines. This advance gave the Philistine army superiority over the Israelites.

How can we distinguish the ethnicity of the material culture of the Israelites in the 12th to 10th century BCE, Iron I period? Shibutani and Kwan (1965, p. 47) suggest that an ethnic group consists of people who conceive of themselves as being alike by virtue of their common ancestry, whether such origin is real or fictitious, and who are so regarded by others. This "we" and "they" perception could consist of territorial or even social boundaries. These boundaries could be expressed by language, rituals, dietary habits, funerary practices, physical features, dress codes, or other cultural behaviors.

The circular and difficult debates over the identity of the early Israelites along the margins of the territories identified from the Biblical text have been challenged over the past 30 years. An example of such a site is Tel Masos, near Be'er Sheva (Figure 4.5), which has been identified as Biblical Hormah and described as Israelite (Fritz and Kempinski 1983; Kochavi and Herzog 1984. Finkelstein (1988, pp. 27-33) suggests defining the ethnic boundaries of early Israelites by two factors: (1) the territorial aspect, using the boundaries of the monarchy in its earliest days and imposing them on the earlier Iron I settlements, since "political unification tends to ultimately have ethnicity creating capabilities," and (2) the socioeconomic aspect, assuming that "Israelite settlements are those sites which were inhabited by newly settled groups."

W. G. Dever (1983) points out that from the late 13th century BCE an ethnic group called itself "Israelite" and was sufficiently well established to be listed as Israel in the aforementioned Merneptah Stele. However, Finkelstein points out that we cannot make any intuitive connection between Israel of 1203 BCE and the area where the Israelite monarchy emerged some years later.

Archaeologists prefer to put ethnic labels on pottery types, but there are, in general, too many variables to establish an ethnos among the Israelite pottery finds. Many of the pottery finds depict trade and cultural influences rather than invasion or political domination. Architecture has also been used as a measure of ethnicity, particularly the four-room Israelite house, but this same

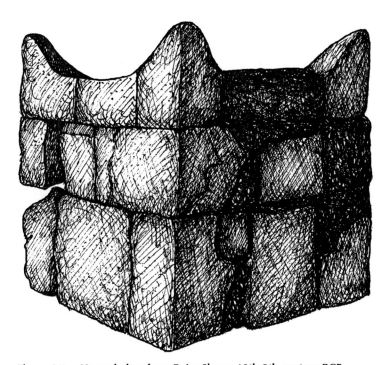

Figure 4.5.   Horned altar from Be'er Sheva, 10th-9th century BCE.

plan has been found in the lowlands and in Transjordan in Iron I sites (Dever 1986, p. 10). Thus it can be concluded that it took centuries until more distinct patterns developed in the ethnicity of the Iron Age I pattern of lifestyle.

The only definite indicator of ethnicity from this period seems to be dietary habits. In their research, Hess and Wapnish show that pigs were not present in proto-Israelite Iron I sites in the highlands, while they were quite numerous in proto-Amorite and Philistine sites. This may evolve into one of the most important clues in identifying ethnicity of the Israelite population in this period (Wapnish 1981, pp. 101-121).

Pig bones make up only 0.9% of the bone assemblages found at Shiloh and may have been intrusive, or brought from elsewhere (Hollwing, Sade and Kishon 1993). No pig bones were found at the Mount Ebal site near Shechem (Kolska and Horwitz 1986-87), or at Khirbet Raddana near Ramallah. At Heshbon in Jordan, southwest of Amman, pigs make up the 4.89% of the faunal remains, or bones (LaBiance 1999, p. 145). In Iron Age I, pigs appear in great numbers in the Shephelah and on the southern coastal plain in areas such as Tel Miqne, Tel Batash and Ashkelon; they are also quite popular at other lowland sites. But they disappear from the bone assemblages of the central hill country. In Iron Age II, pigs continue to be represented in assemblages in Heshbon in Transjordan. As predicted by Stager, pig bones are emerging as the main, if not the only factor, that can shed light on ethnic boundaries in the Iron I period in Canaan.

Dever (2003, pp. 192-193) discusses five points that define Israelite ethnicity by utilizing Fredrik Barth's 1969 work, *Ethnic Groups and Boundaries*. Barth defines an ethnic group as a people who:

1. are biologically self-perpetuating;
2. share a fundamental, recognizable, relatively uniform set of cultural values including language;
3. constitute a partly independent "interaction sphere";
4. have a membership that defines themselves as well as being defined by others, as a category distinct from other categories of the same order; and
5. perpetuate their self-identity both by developing rules for maintaining ethnic boundaries as well as for participating in inter-ethnic social borders.

It appears that the ethnicity of the Iron Age I hill country conforms to most of the above criteria.

From the 15th century until the late 12th century BCE, Beit She'an was an important Egyptian garrison town. By the 11th century, the town was rebuilt on an earlier plan, which was indicative of Canaanite culture. It appears that the local people rehabilitated the town after the Egyptians were expelled.

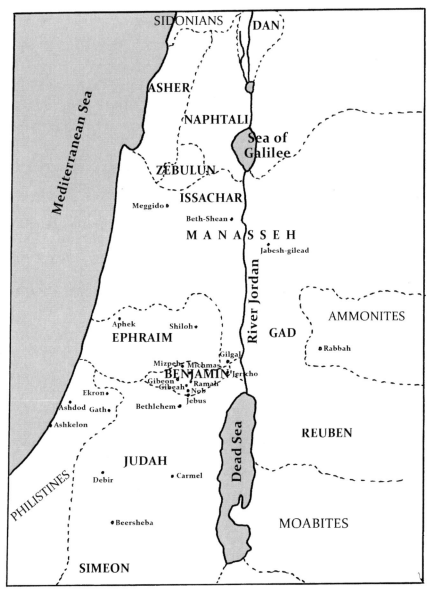

Figure 4.6. Territories of the Tribes of Israel, 11th century BCE.

Beit She'an is mentioned in the Biblical text (I Kings 4:12) and is noted in Shishak's wall relief at Karnak, which documents his violently destructive route from the Jordan Valley to Megiddo in the early 10th century BCE (Mazar 1990, pp. 150-163).

The changes mentioned reflect a continual process of the indigenous population incorporating itself into the evolving Israelite peoplehood. In 1979 N. K. Gottwald, a noted Biblical scholar, published *The Tribes of Yahweh: A Sociology of the Religion of Liberated Israel, 1250-1050 BCE*. His concept was that this process was more of a religious upheaval on the part of the local Canaanite peasants who revolted against their "landlords" and formed a new society based on religious ideology and spirituality (Figure 4.6). They may have been influenced by itinerant Egyptians who brought with them the earlier monotheism of Akhenaten, the 14th -century BCE ruler of Egypt. Whatever the varied reasons were, they caused these groups to come together as followers of one god in direct opposition to the pantheon of the local Canaanite kings, eventually becoming the Israelites.

Archaeological finds also take into account agricultural developments that appear in Canaan, such as the use of iron implements in farming and the quarrying of water cisterns. Economies developed which caused the population to grow in the highlands, attracting outsiders who adapted themselves to the mores and customs of the local inhabitants. Since population growth occurred over a period of perhaps 200 years, there is no evidence of a million or more people suddenly invading the land, as would have been the case if there had been a massive arrival of the Israelite people. Rather, it seems that there was an internal population growth during a period of calm from 1200 BCE to 1000 BCE. The "new nation" was by and large created from within, and therefore its people were entitled to the land that the redactors tell us was given to them by God. The theory of a radical Conquest, as recorded in the Biblical account, is not represented in the archaeological record. Rather, we see a peaceful migration model engaging an internal indigenous population that led to the development of a mix of Canaanite and Israelite cultures over a period of approximately 200 years.

Chapter Five

The Monarchy
Saul, David, and Solomon

Ahad Ha'am, 1856-1927, Jewish philosopher and essayist, said the following:

> Surely it is obvious that the real great men of history, the men, that is, who have become a force in the life of humanity, are not actual, concrete persons who existed in a certain age. There is not a single great man in history of whom the popular fancy has not drawn a picture entirely different from the actual man; and it is this imaginary conception, created by the masses, to suit their needs, and their inclinations, that is the real great man, exerting an influence which abides in some cases for thousands of years–this and not the concrete original, who lived a short time in the actual world, and was never seen by the masses in his true likeness.

Following the Biblical narrative in an attempt to differentiate history from folklore, archaeological facts from scribal propaganda, and memories from living traditions, it is necessary to trace the evolution of the period of the Monarchy and the first memorable kings: Saul, David, and Solomon (Figure 5.1).

After the unstable period of the Judges, the Israelites demanded and were prepared to accept a king. The story of King Saul and his tragic relationship with David is a human story with a passionate interplay of personalities, all within the scope of religious dramas that are the hallmark of the Biblical account. It was a time of extreme crisis throughout Canaan. The Philistine army had devastated the area as was evidenced by early excavations at Tel Qasile (the first official archaeological excavation by the state of Israel in 1948), Tel Aphek, and Ekron. In 1996 the excavation of Tel Miqne, approximately 20 miles west of Jerusalem, produced written confirmation of its status as the Philistine city of Ekron, in the form of an inscription identifying Ikausu, ruler of Ekron, as the builder of a temple erected there around 700 BCE.

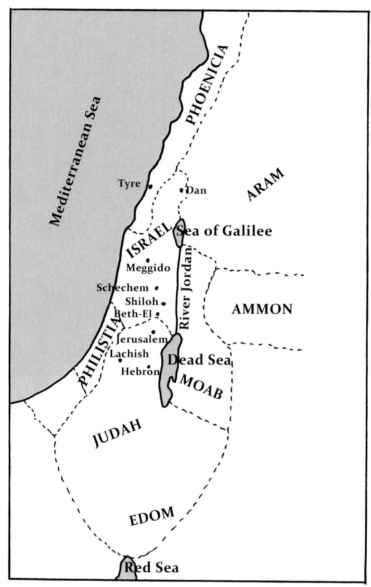

Figure 5.1. Judah and Israel at the time of the Monarchy, 10th-8th century BCE.

Seymour Gitin, director of the American School of Archaeology in Jerusalem, and co-director Dr. Trude Dothan confirm that the inscription indicates that the inhabitants of Ekron retained their ethnic identity as Philistines until the Babylonians destroyed the city in 603 BCE. "There are five rulers of the Philistines, those of Gaza, Ashdod, Ashkelon, Gath and Ekron," says Joshua 13:3. The prophet Amos (circa 750 BCE) wrote, "I will turn my hand against Ekron and the remnants of the Philistines will perish" (Amos 1:18). Excavations at Tell es-Safi, the site of ancient Gath, reveal major destruction at the end of the 9th century BCE. Gath had previously been one of the most important cities in the Shephelah and perhaps the largest city in all of Canaan at the time. A century later it was a small village under the control of Ashdod. How then could it parallel the accounts of David's rise to power unless there was a communal memory of actual past events?

The Egyptian empire had lost its power by the 12th century BCE, marking the end of Egyptian sovereignty over Canaan. The Israelite cities then in existence were governed by tribal and clan-based authorities that were later replaced by a centralized monarchy. Much tension arose between this centralized rule and the tribal chiefs. Judges 17:6 and 18:1 state that "there was no king in Israel; everyone did what was right in his own eyes." A strong sense of tribal unity existed, and only when tribal security was threatened were local alliances realigned. Not until the 10th century BCE, with the total collapse of Egyptian control of these cities, did the population begin to recognize that the centralized authority of a king could defend borders and stabilize their lives.

Saul, the first king, could hardly maintain tribal alliances and could not organize a standing army or sustain a court system. The historical existence of Saul is not documented in any ancient inscriptions or in the chronologies of the neighboring states. Archaeological evidence is only an assumption, based on references from the time frame during which he was supposed to reign. "Saul began to reign and reigned two years over Israel" (I Samuel 13:1). In fact, it is usually assumed that Saul ruled for 22 years, probably between 1030-1010 BCE, since the unclear listing of "two years" would not have fit the timeline or his exploits. These less-than-clear dates have led to some misinterpretations of material finds from excavation.

Saul was a Benjaminite by birth, the son of Kish, and most of his activity takes place in his tribal territory, as well as in adjacent areas and the region to the north. This basically was his kingdom, as nowhere in the Biblical account did he take action in the highlands of Judah, except for his pursuit of David. Ramah, Mizpah, Jib, Michmash, and Givon are all located in the highlands of Benjamin, just north of Jerusalem. It is not difficult to perceive that the Biblical recounting is biased against Saul. His relationship with David is the result of the redactor's use of propaganda to favor David. Saul's personality, his pathological jealousy of David, and his instability should be understood to be part of this bias. Glorifying David and vilifying Saul are part of the epic of the monarchy and should not be considered historical.

All of the imperial powers that surrounded this small kingdom were consumed with their own internal problems. This gave the coalescing tribes of Israel a unique opportunity to cast off foreign domination and form a mini-empire of their own in the process (Kugel 2007, p. 448).

It appears as if Saul is a chieftain who holds court under a tree (I Samuel 2:26). Despite this simple status, Saul was able to unite the Israelite tribes and incorporate the indigenous people into his populace. Until his death the people were loyal to him. This created problems for David when he took the throne, which led, in turn, to the scribes' efforts to legitimize the reign of David. The redactors of these events in historical reporting accept the reality of the moment when they record: "Saul speaks out—'I know that you shall surely be King and the Kingdom of Israel shall be established in your hand'" (I Samuel 24:20).

An additional historical saga from the 10th century BCE is found in the Sheshonq I relief from the Temple of Amun in Karnak in Upper Egypt. The relief is usually associated with the reign of King Rehoboam. Sheshonq I was pharaoh during the Twenty-second dynasty and ruled in the 10th century BCE during the Twenty-second dynasty, just as Egypt lost its power in the area of present-day Israel. Sheshonq I has been identified by some scholars as Shishak, the attacker of Jerusalem and the Temple (I Kings 14:25-26). He embarked on a military incursion into Canaan as recorded on the relief that celebrates his victorious campaign, and includes the place names of the conquered cities. Neither Jerusalem nor Judah is mentioned as having been captured, though both should have been prime targets. However, the relief mentions several villages located in a large cluster north of Jerusalem that were attacked in the course of Sheshonq's campaign. These cities comprised the stronghold of Saul, especially Givon, which Egypt wanted to dismantle since it was seen as a threat to Egyptian influence in the area. David was already the fugitive leader of a band of marauders who had made an alliance with the Philistines. The Egyptian alliance with the Philistines could have been concurrent, making clear the meaning of "the enemy of my enemy is my friend." Once the Egyptians withdrew, David could move north, as it was the Philistines who defeated Saul at Mount Gilboa and hung him and his sons on the wall of Beit She'an (I Samuel 31:10).

It appears that David sat on the sidelines during the Sheshonq I campaign when the Egyptians set out to crush Saul's forces at Aphek. A decline of power in the northern highlands and the settlements of Benjamin where Saul had been the strongest would have given David the opportunity to expand his control in those areas as the Egyptians withdrew. Since neither Philistine cities nor Jerusalem are mentioned in the Sheshonq I list at Karnak, and the cities of Judah were not affected, David's chance of creating a united monarchy from Jerusalem could be realized. The Biblical narrative also gives David the opportunity to opt out of the conflict as the Philistines accused him of double loyalty (I Samuel 29:3-10). However, David praises Saul and his sons in the beautiful liturgy of II Samuel 1:19-25. The struggle between Saul and David blossomed in the historical consciousness of the redactors and became part of a national tradition. This forged a new beginning in the 10th century BCE to heal differences, share a common identity, and forge a new nation.

The account of David's rise to power cannot be corroborated by historical and/or archaeological remains. Three conflicting and irreconcilable stories about David are found in the Bible. In I Samuel 16:1-13, David is secretly anointed by Samuel as king-to-be, which is part of Samuel's rejection of Saul. The second incident is found in I Samuel 16:14-23, when David the harpist is summoned to Saul's court to soothe the king's melancholy spirits. The third story, and the one most frequently repeated, is when David is transformed from shepherd boy to folk hero when he kills the Philistine giant Goliath with one stone from his trusty slingshot, an event that also marks the beginning of Saul's jealousy toward him (I Samuel 17:49). However, in II Samuel 21:19, the credit for killing Goliath goes to Elhanan, the son of Jair of Bethlehem.

In spite of Saul's mistrust, David still wins the hand of Saul's daughter Michal and becomes a commander in Saul's army. Saul's increasing jealousy toward David causes him to flee from the court, making him a fugitive and an outlaw. He takes refuge in Ein Gedi and assembles a tight band of armed followers. This stronghold was excavated in 1949 and again in 1960 by Benjamin Mazar. The excavations revealed that the site was not inhabited until late in the 7th century BCE, nearly 400 years later, which coincides with the time when the interplay between Saul and David was probably written down by a scribe.

David's rise to stardom commences with the murders of Eshbaal, the last heir to Saul's throne, and his commander, Abner. With that, any dynastic claim of the house of Saul to the throne collapsed. David had already been elected king of the southern state of Judah when the northern tribes of Israel invited him to be their king as well (II Samuel 5:1-5). All these events depend on the fact that the house of David existed historically and, therefore, that King David lived! Perhaps he did not exist in the same exaggerated manner that the Biblical account portrays him, and not to the extent of the size of his empire, but we can say that there was a King David! It is impossible to conceive that the scribes imagined such a larger-than-life character. Rather, they embellished the account that came down to them, so that it stood on its own merit throughout the generations. However, the work of the scribes begs the questions of the accuracy and historicity of the saga as opposed to the archaeology and historical events.

The most significant archaeological find to be connected with David came to light during the summer of 1993 at the excavation site in the ancient city of Dan in northern Israel. A stone fragment measuring 12.6 by 8.6 inches was found in a new wall in the town square and was dated to the 9th century BCE. The inscription on the basalt stone was in Aramaic and was very legibly engraved, each word separated by a dot. Two other fragments were found at a later time, and together they make up what is known as the Tel Dan Stele (Figure 5.2). Preserved in moderate condition, 13 engraved lines on the stele suggest a triumphal inscription, a royal proclamation most likely commemorating Hazael, the ruler of Aram Damascus, who is mentioned in Assyrian and Biblical records of the late 9th century BCE. When epigrapher Joseph Naveh and Avraham Biran, the chief archaeologist at the site, translated the inscription, they found this passage on the ninth and tenth lines: "[I] killed [Ahaz]iahu son of [Jehoram] King of the house of David and I set [their towns in ruins and turned] their land into [desolation] . . . ." The Tel Dan Stele records the territorial conflict between Israel and Aram Damascus, as well as Hazael's pursuit of an offensive attack against his southern enemies (Finkelstein and Silberman 2007, pp. 264-265). In this inscription dated approximately 835 BCE, Hazael proclaims that he has killed Jehoram (or the son of Jehoram), the king of Israel, along with Jehoram's ally, the king of the House of David. The Tel Dan Stele contains the oldest non-Biblical, Semitic-language reference to Israel, as well as the earliest non-Biblical mention of the House of David. "It provides an independent witness to the historical existence of a dynasty founded by a ruler named David from just a few generations after the era in which he presumably lived" (Finkelstein and Silberman 2007, p. 266).

The saga of King David as it has come down to us is portrayed in real-life events, unlike the typical biographies of the neighboring kings. His weaknesses, sexual urges, and lewd dances are not hidden; nor is it concealed that he stole another man's wife and planned the execution of her husband. He mourns the death of his son, Avshalom, despite the fact that Avshalom had tried to kill him in his old age. He becomes obsessed with his beautiful, young companion as senility overtakes him. He is forbidden to build the Temple because the blood of his enemies is on his hands. This story is as real as the acts of modern rulers, especially in the Third World, and leads one to believe that David's story was written or at least transcribed close to the period of its portrayal. It gives an air of credence to the detailed court history found in II Samuel 8:16-17.

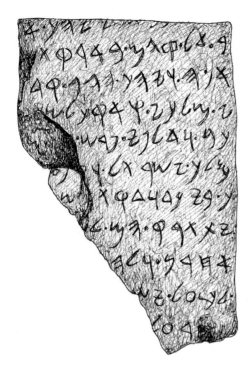

Figure 5.2. Tel Dan Stele with the "House of David" inscription, 9th-8th century BCE.

The Biblical account seems to be concerned mainly with explaining how all of David's sons were disqualified from ruling, with the exception of Solomon, his son by Bathsheba, who was acclaimed king on the day of David's death. At the same time another of his sons, Adonijah, was proclaiming himself king.

David's primary accomplishment was the establishment of a united Hebrew monarchy for the first time, with Jerusalem as the religious and political capital of Israel. After reigning from Hebron for seven years, he set out to take the Jebusite city which lay between Judah and Israel. It became David's royal city, Jerusalem, which like Washington DC today was not aligned with either state.

Jerusalem was separated from the Temple Mount by the Ophel, an uninhabited area that became the government center under Israelite rule. During the reign of Hezekiah, the city walls expanded westward, enclosing the open area on the Western Hill, now known as the Old City. A wealth of archaeological sites in this area of Jerusalem include Hezekiah's Tunnel, Warren's Shaft (an earlier structure thought to be part of a water system, named for British engineer Sir Charles Warren), the Pool of Siloam, and the recently discovered Second Temple pool. The Gihon Spring, found on the lower slope of the Ophel Hill, is the source of these water systems, and its location is one of the reasons given for the development of the city of Jerusalem.

There is a long history of excavation activity in this area, including work by R. A. S. Macalister, Dame Kathleen Kenyon, Yigal Shilo, Ronny Reich, and currently Eilat Mazar. In 2007 Mazar reported the discovery of a monumental structure dating from 1000 BCE, the period of King David. Found at the high point of the city, south of the Temple Mount, its location suggested that this might have been the palace built by David that is described in the fifth chapter of II Samuel. It is important to note that this structure is floating on fill. That is, it was not built on bedrock and there is no occupational level. The supporting stonework is massive, and while it is a major installation, material finds from the 9th century BCE are lacking. Two seal impressions (bullae) from the site, bearing the names of royal ministers mentioned in the book of Jeremiah (38:1), were revealed. The name of Yehucal Ben Shelamiah had been found on another bullae during the excavation season in 2005. That name appears again, along with Gedaliah Ben Pashchur. This was the first time in Israeli archaeology that two clay bullae with Biblical names from the same verse in a primary Biblical source were found in the same site. To date, no verifiable royal tombs have been found in the city of David.

Recently a rather scathing article by Robert Draper, "Kings of Controversy," appeared in *National Geographic* magazine (December 2010, pp. 66-91), contrasting the maximalist views of Eilat Mazar, archaeologist at the City of David excavations, with the minimalist position of Israel Finkelstein of Tel Aviv University and David Ilan of Hebrew Union College. Maximalists are generally traditionalists who accept the Biblical account and its chronology as factual, while minimalists are critical of the historicity of the Bible and the more conventional time frames. The article noted that the City of David excavations are being funded by two organizations, the Shalem Center and the City of David Foundation, both of which are known to be religiously oriented and politically influential. Many archaeologists scoff at the reports coming out of this excavation, contending that they are "throwbacks" to the old school of Biblical archaeology.

Proponents of low chronology (the minimalists) suggest that we "think of the Bible the way you would a stratified archaeological site. Some of it was written in the eighth century BC, some in the seventh, and then going all the way to the second century BC. That is 600 years of compilation. This doesn't mean that the story doesn't come from antiquity. But the reality presented in the story is a later reality. David, for example, is a historical figure. He did live in the tenth century BC. I accept descriptions of David as some sort of leader in an upheaval group, troublemakers who lived on the margins of society. But not the golden city of Jerusalem, not the descriptions of a great empire in the time of Solomon. When the authors of the text describe that they have in their eyes the reality of their own time, the Assyrian Empire" (quoted in Draper 2010).

Mount Moriah is where David purchased a piece of land, a threshing floor mentioned in the Biblical account. This high place, outside the walls of the city of David, cost him fifty shekels of silver, and there David built an altar unto the Lord (II Samuel 24:24). Solomon later consummates this part of the Biblical narrative by building the First Temple on the same site. Mount Moriah is the place where the legends and traditions of three great religions come together: it is where the sacrifice of Isaac, or Ishmael, traditionally took place; where Herod would expand the Second Temple approximately 1,000 years later; and where Jesus was said to have encountered the money changers. Also, it was on Moriah that Mohammed was said to have ascended to Heaven and where the present mosque (the Haram esh Sherif, or the Dome of the Rock) was built in 691 CE.

Solomon's reign began in 970 BCE. He began working on the First Temple in the fourth year of his reign and the structure took some seven and one-half years to complete (I Kings 6:1). After all the words that have been written about the Temple, nothing now remains, and not one trace of its fabled splendor has been found. Even though it lasted 400 years before its destruction by Nebuchadnezzar, not a single building stone has been recovered, even in secondary use. There are no references to Solomon's Temple outside the Bible, and all that is known is derived from descriptions found primarily in I Kings and II Chronicles, neither of which is contemporary with Solomon's reign. The first book of Kings was written about four hundred years after Solomon, following the destruction of the First Temple, and Chronicles was set down considerably later. Attempts have been made to reconstruct models of the First Temple, but the Biblical accounts are more fanciful than factual. Even though many measurements are given, architectural details are lacking. Archaeological excavations at other temple sites give some evidence that Solomon's basic structure could have been modeled on an older Canaanite prototype (Magnusson 1955).

Although the building of the First Temple was the major enterprise of Solomon's reign, it is also recorded that he constructed a magnificent palace made from cedars of Lebanon over a period of 13 years, as well as a judgment hall and a palace for a daughter of the Egyptian pharaoh, one of his 700 wives. In addition, he undertook a massive building program in Ezion Geber, which is next to Eloth (modern-day Elat) on the north end of the Gulf of Aqaba. This construction included a seaport as well as a large number of ships. All of this was accomplished with the assistance of King Hiram of Tyre, who provided the material and craftsmen for the work on the Temple

Mount and other projects. Solomon and Hiram formed a commercial alliance in which Solomon provided harbor facilities for Hiram, who in turn supplied the naval personnel and expertise to develop trade with the Far East. This provided a large income from toll charges (I Kings 9:26-28). However, this partnership as described in the Bible could not have occurred, since Hiram of Tyre did not exist until 738 BCE when we find his name in Tiglath Pileser III's list, more than 200 years later than the building of Solomon's Temple (Grabbe 2007, p. 134).

In 1938-1940 Nelson Glueck of the Hebrew Union Institute claimed that Tell el-Kheleifeh was Solomon's port of Ezion-Geber, but when no remains were found, he abandoned the site. Dr. Beno Rotenberg of Tel Aviv University suggested in 1956-1957 that Coral Island in the Gulf of Aqaba was a more likely contender for the site of Biblical Ezion-Geber. Ten years later, an expedition from the Undersea Exploration Society of Israel spent three seasons exploring the area in a joint Anglo-Israeli effort which proved inconclusive. There were no shipwrecks, artifacts, or harbor installations that could be dated to the 10th century BCE.

If this harbor had actually been built, the romantic saga of the Queen of Sheba and Solomon (I Kings, chapters 10-15) might have happened differently. Such a large seaport would have given good access to Africa and the Orient. The queen's journey over 1,500 miles of rough terrain, accompanied by camels laden with precious gifts for Solomon, would have been more easily accomplished by ship. This would have been logical if indeed the harbor was in existence. There are no signs of the ostentatious wealth mentioned in this romantic legend that can be connected with any of the Solomonic sites. It is an exaggerated story, written about 500 years after Solomon's time to glorify his kingship.

The cities of Megiddo, Gezer, and Hazor are most frequently associated with the grandeur of David and Solomon's empire. All three sites were extensively excavated in the 1950s, when Biblical archaeology was in vogue. Megiddo was one of the most important cities in Biblical Israel. First excavated in the second and third decades of the 20th century by the Oriental Institute of the University of Chicago, large sections of the remains were attributed to Solomon's builders (9th century BCE). At stratum IV, two large buildings with long rows of chambers divided into three aisles separated by partition walls and troughs were identified as Solomon's Stables, described in the Biblical text (I Kings 9:15).

When Professor Yigael Yadin excavated Hazor in the 1950s, he found a large city gate dated to the Iron Age period. It was similar to the six-chambered gate that was excavated at Megiddo in the 1930s, and Yadin believed that the Hazor gate was also from the time of Solomon. When he examined the excavation reports of R.A. S. Macalister from the beginning of that century and found exactly the same gate plan, Yadin assumed that this must have been the master plan for a Solomonic city. This type of archaeological basis for dating the period of David and Solomon is the result of badly mistaken calculation (Finkelstein and Silberman 2002, p. 140).

The use of Philistine pottery as a dating tool is not possible during this period, since apparently this type of ceramic did not continue into the 10th century BCE. New research into pottery types and forms shows that the so-called Solomonic levels at Megiddo, Gezer, and Hazor belong to the early 9th century BCE, nearly 100 years after the death of Solomon. New methods in carbon-14 dating now produce solid evidence and reduce the margin of error in chronology.

At Megiddo, samples from fifteen wooden beams were thought to be from the time of Solomon. Carbon-dating results confirm that the dates are much later than originally thought. Parallel dating from other sites using carbon-14 helps to anchor a new dating. There has been a misdating of both Davidic and Solomonic remains by almost a full century, which helps to explain why Jerusalem and Judah are so lacking in material finds of the 10th century BCE.

There is no archaeological indication of monumental architecture in Jerusalem from the time of David and Solomon in the 10th century BCE that would be expected in a major city. This holds true for Megiddo, Gezer, and Hazor as well. There was very little changed in the north and the Canaanite material culture continued. The area was mainly rural with about 250 sites that have been recorded by archaeologists. No written documents, inscriptions, or signs of literacy have been found, and it is difficult to identify a centrally administered state north of Jerusalem, while the south was sparsely populated. Jerusalem was a typical highland village. Population estimates suggest that 45,000 people lived in the hill country, 90% of whom resided in villages in the north. Perhaps 5,000 people were scattered between Jerusalem, Hebron, and an additional 20 small villages. "Archaeologically, we can say no more about David and Solomon except that they existed, and their legend endures" (Finkelstein and Silberman 2007, p. 17). The familiar stories about David and Solomon based on a few early folk traditions are the result of extensive reworking and editorial expansion during the four centuries that followed the reigns of David and Solomon.

Chapter Six

The Divided Kingdom
to the First Exile

With the fall of the United Monarchy, we now confront the new reality of two kingdoms: Judah in the south and Israel in the north. The sequence of events leading to this reality occurred in a dramatically different version than the one described in the Bible. In the two hundred years following the death of Solomon, the configuration of Israel and Judah changed significantly.

Jeroboam I, described in the Biblical text as "a mighty man of valor" (I Kings 11:28), led the Northern Kingdom of Israel out of the union with Judah almost immediately after Solomon's death around 920 BCE. After a long period of centralized government in Jerusalem, and prosperity for both the north and the south, the tribes of the northern hill country and the Galilee began to resist the demands for forced labor that were begun by Solomon and intensified by his son Rehoboam. This situation eventually led to a split between Judah and Israel. The result was a resurgence of violence and idolatry in the Northern Kingdom.

The northern hill country of Israel dominates the last days of the United Monarchy, while the Judean highland areas were weaker until the collapse of the Northern Kingdom in 722 BCE. Scholars have used portions of the Biblical account verbatim, as if these events actually happened as described. This is not the case. With population increases, these two entities reveal an interplay of social development out of rural isolation, pastoralists giving way to settled farming, and villages becoming part of urbanization. While both communities grew in size, the northern hill country had a more populated settlement area than the south. The pattern of Israel versus Judah and Shechem versus Jerusalem slowly emerged. Due to its geographical location, Judah was able to maintain its national identity. It had the advantage of being hill country, far from the main trade routes and had Israel on the north as a buffer against Assyrian destruction.

During the 1980s the Israel Antiquities Authority conducted surveys in the northern areas that brought to light settlement patterns of the 10th and 9th centuries BCE. Judah was made up of approximately 20 small villages, while Israel in the north had dozens of sites with a well-developed settlement system and large regional centers. In other words, Israel was booming.

Jeroboam fortified Shechem as the new capital of Israel. Although there seemed to have been many skirmishes between Israel and Judah, the real enemy was Egypt, then ruled by Sheshonq I. Earlier in this volume the epic encounter of the Biblical Sheshonq (actually Pharaoh Sheshonq I of the Twenty-second dynasty) with King David was addressed. Most Biblical scholars associate Shishak/Sheshonq with the devastation of both Judah and Israel in the late 10th century BCE. However, Egypt did not occupy this area, but only wanted to destabilize it. The archaeological record is not clear on the date of this intrusion, but it would be remiss not to bring this episode to mind again.

In order to consolidate his position as king, Jeroboam had to establish an official religious cult to rival that of Jerusalem's Temple in the south. I Kings 12:27 relates "If this people go up to do sacrifice in the house of the Lord in Jerusalem, then shall the heart of this people turn again unto their Lord, even unto Rehoboam King of Judah and they shall kill me [Jeroboam] and go again to Rehoboam." To counter the Jerusalem Temple, Jeroboam set up two cult sanctuaries, one in Dan on the extreme northern border of Israel and the second at Beth El, 12 miles north of Jerusalem.

Jeroboam ruled for 22 years. When he died, his son and successor Nadab (909-908) was overthrown by a military coup in which all the surviving members of the house of Jeroboam were killed. King Baasha reigned until 885 before he was also killed and Zimri, an army commander, lasted just seven days as ruler. Finally Omri, the head of the army, was chosen by the people to be the next king. Omri (884-874 BCE) succeeded in stabilizing the Northern Kingdom after its first turbulent decade. He and his son Ahab (873-852 BCE) brought the kingdom of Israel to the peak of its strength and political importance. Omri restored stable government and reduced tension with Jerusalem by marrying his daughter Athaliah to the king of Judah. Omri also cemented an alliance with the Phoenicians with the marriage of Ahab to Jezebel, a Phoenician princess. He reigned for 12 years, and built a new capital at Samaria (Finkelstein and Silberman 2002, p. 172).

Despite Omri's successful endeavors, the prejudicial accounts in the Bible make it sound as though Omri and Ahab brought the "new" kingdom to its ruin. Again, it is important to recall that the scribes at the time when the Bible was written were aligned with Jerusalem-oriented priests.

It is at this point, in the period of Omri and Ahab, that we have an inter-face with contemporary records from a neighboring state. The black basalt Moabite Mesha Stele, inscribed with an account of King Mesha's struggle against Israel, was found in 1868 in the village of Dhiban by the Reverend F. A. Klein, a Prussian missionary. This site is on the east side of the Dead Sea, which is referred to as Moab in the Bible. The stele was destroyed by the villagers shortly after Klein returned to France. Fortunately, he had made a wax mold from which the stele was restored; it is now on display in the Lou-vre. The inscription tells us that Israel extended at that time further east and south of its earlier heartland in the central hill country. The 34-line text was written in approximately 830 BCE to commemorate King Mesha's victory over the Israelites in his battle for freedom. "I will humble Moab . . . while Israel hath perished forever." The inscription was written in the Moabite language, which is related to Biblical Hebrew. Mesha is mentioned in the third chapter of II Kings as a rebellious vassal of the Northern Kingdom of Israel. This stele is one of the earliest historical descriptions, apart from the Biblical narrative, of the Omride dynasty. Omri had taken possession of the land of Medeba, where he built two cities, Ataroth and Jahaz, as recorded in the Mesha Stele.

The "House of David" inscription was discovered in 1993 in the Dan excavations on Israel's northern border. It describes how King Hazael, ruler of Aram Damascus, captured the city of Dan and erected a triumphal stele there around 835 BCE. Carved in the stele is the accusation that the king of Israel entered into Hazael's land, which suggests that Israel, under Omri, expanded its territories from Damascus through the central highlands to the southern territory of Moab. Another important ancient text, the Monolith In-scription, was found in 1835 by English explorer Austen Henry Layard at the Assyrian site of Nimrod. It relates that Shalmaneser, the Assyrian king, led a major invasion to capture Syria, Phoenicia, and Israel. These three countries mounted stiff resistance, with Israel contributing 2,000 chariots and 10,000 foot soldiers. Although Shalmaneser claimed victory, the Assyrian advance to the west was halted. Yet the Biblical account says little about the power of the Omride kingdom. The text mentions only the elaborate palaces in Samaria and Jezreel.

Excavations at Samaria have revealed the Omride royal city with its el-evated platform and elaborate palace, demonstrating the wealth and power of this reign. At Megiddo in the 1920s, a team from the Oriental Institute of the University of Chicago excavated an Iron Age palace that was similar to the palace at Samaria. John Crowfoot, leader of the expedition to Samaria, was also on the team with the Oriental Institute. He recognized the parallels in the architecture and made the supposition that both had been built by the Omrides. However, the Megiddo team was more inclined maintain the earlier dating, placing their palace during the United Monarchy of David and Solomon. When Yigael Yadin uncovered another palace in Megiddo in the early 1960s, he attributed both of them to Solomon, while dating the later levels which included the stables and other structures to the Omrides. This dating was later re-evaluated to an even later period. The lack of acknowledgement of the impressive architectural achievements of the Omrides was typical of the field of Biblical archaeology in the mid-1900s. The Biblical account had more credence in the public eye than the actual archaeological finds.

Excavations at Tel Dan, directed by Avraham Biran of the Hebrew Union Institute, uncovered a large Iron Age sanctuary with a high altar and extensive fortifications. A large podium constructed of beautifully dressed ashlars was correctly dated to the Omride dynasty. At Megiddo and Hazor, large underground water tunnels cut through the bedrock are some of the most impressive remains from the time of the Omrides. To facilitate the delivery of water to the city, large vertical shafts, approximately 100 feet deep, were constructed with supporting walls. At Hazor a sloping tunnel 80 feet long led into a chamber that held underground water, while at Megiddo a horizontal tunnel extending more than 200 hundred feet led to a cave with a natural spring. Yigael Yadin dated both water systems to the time of the Omrides due to similar architectural detail and their massive construction.

The most revealing site of the Omride period is Jezreel, ten miles east of Megiddo in the Jezreel Valley. The excavation by David Ussishkin of Tel Aviv University and John Woodhead of the British School of Archaeology in Jerusalem brought to light a large compound with similarities to the royal compound in Samaria. What was most unusual was that this compound was inhabited for only a short period of time in the 9th century BCE before it was destroyed. Since it was occupied so briefly, it was not contaminated by other occupation. Because of this unique situation, the site is used to date Omride occupation. It is assumed that it was destroyed with the defeat of the Omrides by the armies of Aram Damascus as they invaded northern Israel. The collection of pottery found at the site was identical to the ceramics that appeared in the palace of Megiddo, which had been attributed to Solomon. Therefore, we can assume that the pottery typology at Megiddo is Omride and not from the period of the Monarchy as previously thought. The other ashlar-type buildings at Jezreel were of the same construction as those in the Samaria compounds. It seems that almost all of the monumental buildings attributed to David and Solomon were actually Omride.

To re-date the period of the Davidic monarchy to the Omrides, approximately 75 to 80 years later, is a startling and emotional upheaval, and it becomes almost an impossible task to gain acceptance for the proposed revision, as it creates a major shift in the traditions that have developed during 3000 years. We must consider, in addition to the ceramic evidence, the architectural parallels and the carbon-14 dating that assigns the destruction of these cities to the time of the Omrides. The cities can now be associated with the campaign of King Hazael of Damascus, which occurred between 835and 800 BCE. During this period at least three of the fortresses at Tel Dan, Hazor, and Beth Saida display Aramean characteristics. In addition, the majority of ostraca (inscribed pottery) carries inscriptions in Aramaic (Finkelstein and Silberman 2002, p. 205).

The first book of Kings describes Ahab (873-852 BCE) as a religious tyrant. However, a monolithic inscription of Shalmaneser depicts Ahab as a strong opponent of Assyrian domination, who sent his mighty chariot forces to face the Assyrians at Qarqar. In this inscription, Shalmaneser boasts of a great victory, but it seems that he must have stopped this campaign, as the Assyrian forces withdrew for a short period in 841 BCE. A year later, after King Jehu (842-814) seized the throne, Shalmaneser III raged through Syria again and into the northern parts of Israel. The famous Black Obelisk depicts Jehu kneeling before the Assyrian king, kissing the ground at his feet. This is the only known portrait of an Israelite king (Figure 6.1).

Tel Tzafit, located on the southern coastal plain, is identified with the Biblical Philistine city of Gat. Dr. Aren Maeir of Bar-Ilan University recently uncovered a horned altar reminiscent of the other horned altars found in Israelite sites (Figure 4.5). Maeir said, "The altar demonstrates the cultural proximity between the Philistines and the Israelites, cast as the most bitter of enemies in the scriptures." He also suggests that the fall of Gat and the weakening of the Philistine kingdom in the south of Israel were factors that supported the rise of the kingdom of Judea and the golden era of the Judean kings in the 9th and 8th centuries BCE (Nir Hasson, *Ha'aretz*, July 26, 2011).

Since the redactors preserved stories and oral traditions from their own points of view, we must depend on the archaeological record for an accurate reading of the history of this period. It is evident that the scribes were trying to write the texts for their own aggrandizement. The writers of the first book of Kings wanted to show the vile side of the Omrides (I Kings 16:25), and they prophesied that the rulers would receive divine punishment for their behavior. That bad conduct was linked to idolatry at the majestic palaces of Jezreel and the profanation of the cult from Jerusalem.

The goal of the scribes was to delegitimize the Omrides and the Northern Kingdom, and to justify the horrible defeat of the Omride family at the hands of the Assyrians. It would be impossible to show the progress of the Northern Kingdom in contrast with the less-developed Southern Kingdom's inability

Figure 6.1. Shalmaneser III relief; the Israelite king Jehu pays tribute to the Assyrian ruler in second panel from top, 9th century BCE.

to expand. It is as if the scribes deflected the grandeur of the Omride period back to the time of David and Solomon. There is now a general agreement that the period of the Omrides shaped the largest and most powerful early Israelite kingdom.

In the middle of the 8th century BCE, trouble once again came from the north. King Tiglath-Pileser II is referred to as Pul in the Bible. He began to reign in 745 BCE, one year after the death of King Jeroboam II of Israel. Israel was plunged into anarchy with a murderous palace coup under King Menahem (747-737 BCE). At the same time Syria was exacting tribute from Israel. Menahem's son Pekahiah (737-735 BCE) was assassinated not long after he succeeded his father, and then Pekah, one of the army commanders, seized the throne and ruled from 735-732 BCE. In 734 BCE, Tiglath-Pileser invaded Israel again. In response, Pekah tried to form a coalition of neighboring states, but Judah, under King Ahaz (743-727) refused to join. Instead he sent messengers to Tiglath-Pileser with silver and gold taken from the

Temple (II Kings 16:7). Archaeological evidence and the Pileser inscription confirm that Pileser destroyed Hazor and Megiddo. The capital, Samaria, was spared when Pekah was assassinated and replaced by a vassal king appointed by Tiglath-Pileser. The rest of Israel was divided into three Assyrian provinces, and large numbers of the inhabitants were exiled to other parts of the empire. Many chose to escape south to Judah. In turn, the Assyrians initiated a transfer plan which brought in conquered populations from other areas to settle Israel: ". . . and they took possession of Samaria and dwelt in it" (II Kings 17:24). This population exchange was far from total. The number of people from the Galilee and from Samaria, which is noted in the Assyrian sources by Tiglath-Pileser III and listed by Sargon II, is about 40,000. This comprises no more than a fifth of the estimated population of the Northern Kingdom west of the Jordan River in the 8th century BCE (Finkelstein and Silberman 2002, p. 221).

King Hiram of Tyre, a name mentioned several times in reference to the building of Solomon's Temple, can be historically connected to the annals of Tiglath-Pileser III (730 BCE), who ruled at the same time as Menahem of Israel (747-737 BCE). It seems that the legendary tales of Solomon were in some manner a way to emphasize the achievements of the Northern Kingdom of Israel after its fall in 722 BCE, along with the rise of David's increasingly prosperous kingdom in the south.

As a result of the transfer of the local population after the Assyrian conquest in 722 BCE, the Samaritans emerge as an ethnic community. They are a mixture of various peoples living in Samaria, according to the Biblical narrative in II Kings, even though the Samaritans themselves claim to be direct descendents of the tribes of Ephraim and Manasseh. Their Temple was constructed on Mount Gerizim, near Shechem, where according to their tradition Abraham was commanded to offer his son Isaac as a sacrifice. Genetic and demographic studies carried out in the 1960s confirm DNA testing results which show that the Samaritans are distinct from other ethnic groups. At the present time only about 700 Samaritans live in Israel.

The cause of Israel's defeat was its success, economically, politically and militarily. In the shadow of the huge Assyrian empire, it was a threat; it was eliminated to add to the prosperity of Assyria's imperial design. Judah was poor and was left as an unattractive destination for the remaining people of Israel.

The smaller kingdom of Judah was ruled from Jerusalem, where the First Temple, an area of centralized worship, was built as a small shrine during the reign of Solomon. He would not have had the resources to construct an elaborate structure like the one described in the book of Kings. The refurbishing of the Temple took place over a period of approximately 100 years from the time of King Jehoash (836-798 BCE) until King Hezekiah (727-698 BCE). No archaeological remains of the First Temple, as described in detail in Kings and Chronicles, can be identified. Not even one foundation stone or ashlar in secondary use has been found. It was only after the conquest of Israel in approximately 720 BCE and the destruction of Samaria that Jerusalem was established as the religious center and experienced a population explosion. At that time the city of David expanded onto the Western Hill (today's Old City). Jerusalem increased in size from a 12-acre town to a city of some 150 acres in the space of one generation. This growth in the size of the population is attested to by the remains that have been uncovered from the vast excavations in the Jewish Quarter since the Six-Day War in 1967.

Much later, in the 1st century BCE, King Herod reconstructed the entire platform of the Temple. If anything remained of the First Temple, it could have been destroyed in the course of these renovations. The author of I Kings 6 described the Temple in detail and probably worshipped there.

The 8th century BCE was dominated in Judah by kings–Ahaz, Hezekiah and Manasseh. According to the archaeological record, Ahaz incorporated Judah into the economy of Assyria and experienced widespread economic growth as a result. The Biblical account describes Ahaz as an evil ruler. His son Hezekiah joined the rebellion against Assyria, which led to the eventual ruin of Judah. Assyria ruled Judah for many years a result of Hezekiah's miscalculation. The Bible describes Hezekiah as one of the most righteous kings of Judah.

The Shephelah (hill country), where this writer has excavated for more than 17 years, was destroyed and abandoned during this period. It was only in the reign of Manasseh, who is listed in the Bible as the most evil king, that Judah was brought back into the economy of Assyria and the Shephelah and the Be'er Sheva region was revitalized.

And what of the nearly 150 years between Jeroboam I and the reign of Jeroboam II? The earlier kings were not as productive as their northern counterparts, even though the Bible portrays them as a blend of the kings of Israel and Judah. There were constant skirmishes between kings of Judah, who could not equal the Northern Kingdom in its ability to expand its territory, build monumental buildings, or raise a powerful army. Lachish was the only city to flourish in the south during this period. Even Jerusalem did not become a religious center until the reign of Hezekiah in the late 7th century BCE. Idolatry was practiced throughout the hill country, attested to by the hundreds of figurines, incense burners, and sacrificial artifacts that have been excavated throughout Judah. The small hill communities had not changed their religion since the early Iron Age.

Prior to the time of Hezekiah (727-698 BCE), the kingdom of Judah went through varying periods of success and failure. There is very little in the way of archaeological evidence, so much of its history is gleaned from the books of Kings. Judah reached its low point almost immediately after the division of the kingdom, when Jeroboam (851-843 BCE) married into the notorious family of Ahab and Jezebel. This event set off a chain reaction leading Athaliah (842-836 BCE) to take the throne and order the death of all the heirs of the house of David. After Athaliah's death, Jehoash reigned in Jerusalem for forty years and ". . . did what was right in the eyes of the Lord all his days" (II Kings 12:2). The kings who came after Jehoash emulated this virtuous behavior, up to the time of King Ahaz (743-727 BCE). His disastrous reign ended when his son Hezekiah became king, ruling for 29 years and initiating sweeping reforms that enhanced the centrality and sanctity of Jerusalem.

Isaiah is one of the prophets from the time of Hezekiah. With 66 chapters, the book of Isaiah spans a historical period of more than 200 years. That amount of time would require the work of at least two authors, and many scholars attribute the chapters to three or more writers. The first 39 chapters consist mainly of condemnations and reconciliations. Chapters 13 to 23 are concerned with the enemies of Israel. The Babylonians, Assyrians, and Philistines were primary but others such as the Egyptians, Syrians, and Edomites are also condemned. However, in Chapter 40 the words "Comfort, O Comfort my people, says your God" (Isaiah 40:11) set a more prophetic tone for the next 20 chapters, suggesting that we are hearing from a new, more visionary writer. Even the style of the writing changes, which indicates the work of other writers in addition to the visionary one.

Much later, during the Judeo-Christian period (1st century CE to the Bar Kokhba revolt in 165 CE), the Messianic movement declared Jesus to be its savior. Isaiah's prophesies (in chapters 42 to 53) offered the "proof" that the writers of the Gospel, the first four books of the New Testament, understood to foreshadow the birth of Jesus. The passage referring to "the servant of the Lord" is seen as a binding element in the relationship between the Hebrew Bible and the Christian Bible. It was imperative that Christianity should not sever its ties with Hebrew scripture, which is the foundation of the New Testament.

The Isaiah Scroll now on display in the Israel Museum in Jerusalem is the oldest known copy of the book of Isaiah. It was transcribed in about 100 BCE, according to paleographic and scribal dating studies, even though carbon-dating tests assign it to the 3rd or 2nd century BCE. The Isaiah Scroll is part of the group of Dead Sea scrolls that were recovered in 1947, and it is the most complete of the more than 200 scrolls found in Qumran Cave I. The Isaiah Scroll measures 24 feet long and almost one foot high with 54 columns of text. Comparisons between the Isaiah Scroll and the much later Masoretic Text (6th to 9th century CE) reveal only small grammatical differences that do not significantly alter the meaning of the text.

It is also important to mention the book of Psalms, which tradition says was authored by King David. In fact, 73 of the Psalms use "L'David" in their titles. However, modern Biblical scholars recognize that this attribution does not necessarily denote authorship, since others could have written the Psalms about David or on his behalf. There is also wide variance in the geographical place of writing; for example, Psalm 137 ("By the waters of Babylon . . .") must have been set down 400 years after David's death. There are also significant differences in language usage among the Psalms, indicating multiple authorship.

Chapter Seven

The Period That Yielded the Bible
Hezekiah through Josiah

The end of the aggressive Northern Kingdom actually served as a catalyst for the growth of the kingdom of Judah. King Ahaz (743-727 BCE) gave up the national identity of Judah and became a vassal king to Assyria. Always aware of his position, he nevertheless launched a massive building program throughout his "country" which coincided with the influx of a new population from the north (Figure 7.1). The previously empty countryside was settled, new towns emerged, and Lachish became a major center as the population increased tenfold. The Be'er Sheva valley expanded with new settlements and trade centers that lay astride the trade route with Arabia. These changes brought economic stabilization, which in turn led to an accumulation of wealth in Jerusalem that supported the training of scribes and priests. Their role was to create a "new" history that would serve as Judah's central scripture and create cohesiveness among the people.

Hezekiah the son of Ahaz is well liked by the Deuteronomic scribes. The second book of Kings states that "he did what was right in the sight of the Lord" (II Kings 18:3). According to scripture, this citation was probably given to him because of his religious reforms which were a reason to "save" him from the Assyrian king Sennacherib in 701 BCE. An Assyrian assault was always a fearful possibility. While Sennacherib was trying to quell the revolt that had taken place in various parts of his empire, Hezekiah made the mistake of joining that revolt. Three years later, after much consolidation, Sennacherib struck Judah with a vengeance. The Sennacherib Prism, a hexagonal clay column found in Nineveh, describes his victorious campaign and includes an account of the siege of Hezekiah's stronghold in Jerusalem. Sennacherib, the writer of the Prism account, describes Hezekiah as "a prisoner, like a bird in a cage," though there is no archaeological evidence of a siege wall or remains of an Assyrian army camp outside the walls of Jerusalem (Figure 7.2).

67

Figure 7.1. Sargon II of Assyria, responsible for deportation of Israelites after capture of Samaria, 720 BCE.

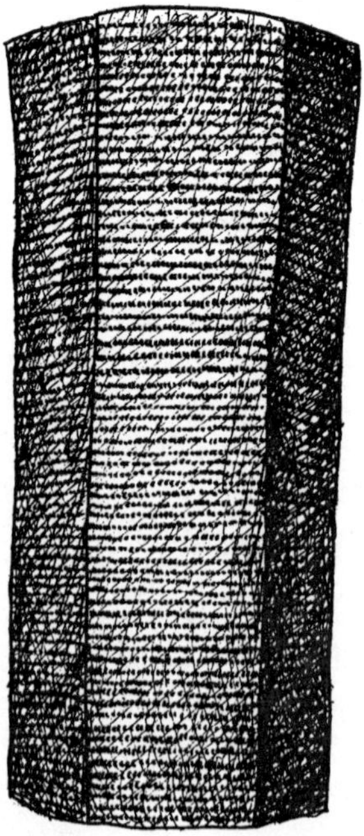

Figure 7.2. Sennacherib Prism: hexagonal clay column. Nineveh, 701 BCE.

The story in II Kings 19:35 is quite different. Although Hezekiah was encouraged by the prophet Isaiah, he refused to yield to Sennacherib. When Sennacherib returned from Lachish, "the angel of the Lord went out and smote in the camp of the Assyrians 185,000, and when they arose early in the morning, behold, they were all dead" (II Kings 19:35). This story is refuted by most historians and considered folklore.

Shortly before this supposed battle for Jerusalem, a crucial event took place at Lachish, approximately five miles south of Jerusalem in the plain of the Shephelah. This battle was the climax of Sennacherib's campaign and he chose it as the subject of a series of carved wall reliefs that are now on display in the British Museum in London. These large panels are very detailed, showing captives executed and hung on the walls of Lachish or being led away to slavery and exile. They also depict Sennacherib watching as Lachish is consumed by flames, an event that caused most of the surviving population in the area to flee to Jerusalem. These panels are considered to be the most graphic documentation of conquest ever found in the ancient world (Magnusson 1977, p. 186).

Evidence of how organized provisions were in the time of Hezekiah has been found in the seals on the handles of large storage jars from Judah. These seal impressions have an emblem in the shape of a winged sun disc or a beetle, with a Hebrew inscription "L'Melech" or "to the king," suggesting that the contents of the containers on which the seals were placed belonged to the king. These seals appear in wide distribution, and three were found by the writer at Tel Maresha (Stern, unpublished dissertation 2002). While the use of the jars on which the seals are found is not certain, they do suggest a high level of organization in Judah before the rebellion against Sennacherib and Assyria.

Several ostraca (pottery shards with writing) are also recorded from this period. The Arad Ostraca and the Lachish Letters (also ostraca) are important examples of archaeological evidence. In 1935 James Starkey, excavating in the guardroom of the city gate in Lachish, found the first of 18 ostraca from this site, all written in cursive Hebrew script. The passage on the pottery fragment ends with the observation that Azekah (a tel within eyesight of Lachish) had just fallen and that Lachish would be next. The writer says, ". . . let the Lord know that we are watching for the fire beacons of Lachish, for they cannot see Azekah . . . ." Seals with names such as Gemaryahu Ben Shaphon, Gedalyahu "who is over The House," Milkomar the servant of Baalisha, and Jaazanial the servant of the king, lend further substance to the archaeological information about this period.

The books of Chronicles were probably written several hundred years after the books of Kings and they describe, in retrospect, the places that Hezekiah ordered reinforced for the imminent Assyrian attack. Warehouses for food and livestock were built across the country. II Chronicles describes Hezekiah's most spectacular engineering project, the construction of the Siloam Tunnel, still recognized as an awesome feat. To accomplish this, Hezekiah stopped the upper water course of the Gihon Spring and brought it straight down to the west side of the city of David (II Chronicles 32:30). It was an extraordinary project, almost a third of a mile long and quite narrow, snaking in an exaggerated S-curve through the solid rock of the Ophel Hill. The meeting of the two teams of diggers was commemorated in an inscription in classical Hebrew, now housed in the Archaeological Museum in Istanbul, Turkey, that originally would have been part of the rock wall of the tunnel (Figure 7.3). New excavations in 2008 have diverted the water once again to make this site more accessible to tourists.

Hezekiah also built a fortification wall, over 20 feet thick, on the Western Hill, a piece of which can be seen today in the modern Jewish Quarter. The wall encircled the city, including the Jewish and Armenian Quarters north of the present Jaffa Gate. With the fall of Israel, Jerusalem experienced an increase in population and this wall served to protect the enlarged population.

According to traditional folklore, the religious reforms of Hezekiah began with the destruction of the Nehushtan, the bronze serpent that Moses had made which had the power to protect people from snakebites. Its destruction was a symbolic act, carried out to appease the priesthood. Hezekiah established the division of the priests and the Levites according to their tasks. The priests who came from the north were of the Aaronid line and probably wrote the priestly sections of the Bible. Baruch Halpern has collected evidence of

Figure 7.3. Siloam Inscription, classical Hebrew. Marks completion of water tunnel and describes the engineering process, 6th century BCE.

an ancient work describing the kings of Judah from Solomon to Hezekiah. This was also a time of great literary activity. The books of Isaiah, Micah, Hosea, and Proverbs were written. Centralization of religion was established for future kings, including Hezekiah's son Manasseh, and Josiah, who was his equal as a reformer. "These narratives were written as a reaction to the destruction of the Temple in Jerusalem, retrojecting current problems into the past and thus, cannot be used for historical reconstruction of 701 BCE but rather of 586 BCE" (Grabbe 2007, p. 197).

Although Hezekiah inherited a unified, wealthy state, Sennacherib destroyed it. Hezekiah's disastrous confrontation with Assyria was a huge mistake. From the period of Hezekiah and Manasseh onward, the gap between the Biblical account and the archaeological record narrows. The Bible now becomes a more reliable source for the historical events of the time.

Hezekiah died in 698 BCE and his 12-year-old son Manasseh took the throne. The Bible portrays Manasseh as a terrible king and his reign as a black period. He is, however, well documented in Assyrian inscriptions. Sennacherib was assassinated in 681 BCE and was succeeded by Esarhaddon (681-669 BCE) who left us many royal inscriptions in which Manasseh, king of Judah, is listed. It appears that Manasseh realized that it was in the best interest of the Assyrians for the small state of Judah to act as a buffer against Egypt and was therefore granted special treatment. His long reign of 45 years was a prosperous and peaceful time for Judah. Along with the increased construction and trade, the territory expanded as a wave of settlements was established in the Be'er Sheva valley, following the trade routes of the southern coastal plain. Two 7th century BCE forts, deep in the desert, are attributed to Manasseh's reign. A Hebrew seal with South Arabian names lends credence to the thought that Manasseh's wife Meshullemeth was an Arabian woman. This could have been a diplomatic marriage and may have served as the basis for the folktale of Sheba visiting Solomon almost 300 years earlier.

However successful Manasseh was in integrating Judah into the economy of Assyria, the scribes of the Bible condemn him for destroying all of his father's religious reforms. According to II Kings 21:16, he spilled the blood of his own people. The archaeological record, however, does not bear this out. That the scribes portrayed him as the wickedest of all kings only attests to the prejudices of the Deuteronomists, who took power for a short period after Manasseh's death in 642 BCE. It seems that Manasseh and his advisors pacified their Assyrian overlords, as Manasseh is mentioned in a group of kings who supplied material for a royal project, and again as one of the kings who helped the next Assyrian king conquer Egypt. He re-established the ritual cult of Baal-Asherah, gaining the confidence of the rural population. Economically he rebuilt his smaller kingdom even though Judah was a vassal of Assyria.

Later in the 7th century BCE Jerusalem had no rivals, yet there is little evidence that the city was an administrative center which would have required large buildings. It may be that the city functioned as a commercial and trading center. At the same time the population in the Judean Hills declined, even though the number of settlements remained practically the same (Ofer 2001).

Manassah was followed on the throne by Amon (641-640 BCE) who was assassinated in Jerusalem after only two years, an event that brought his young son Josiah (various sources give his age as three or eight years old) to the throne. Josiah (639-609 BCE) reigned for 31 years and is praised as the most righteous king, rivaling King David himself. In fact, Josiah is represented as the quintessential example of a king and is probably the model for the grandeur that is attributed to David. During his reign the Jerusalem priests and scribes flourished, leaving us the history they devised based on current events. These writings were later redacted into the Hebrew Bible. II Kings 23:25 sings the praises of Josiah at a level that surpasses all other kings. He is portrayed as the hope for national redemption.

According to Biblical historians, when Josiah was 18, he received a message that the High Priest Hilkiah had found a scroll during the refurbishing of the Temple in Jerusalem in 622 BCE (II Kings 23:2-3). When Shaphan, the scribe, read the text, Josiah rent his clothing in anguish as he recognized that the scribe was reading from the "Book of the Law." Scholars who hold the view that the completion of the Bible began no later than the reign of King Josiah suggest that the "Book of the Law" given to Josiah (II Kings 22:10-20 and II Chronicles 34:14-31) was actually an early version of Deuteronomy. It was during Josiah's reign that priests and scribes began compiling the Torah, along with the books of Joshua, Judges, Samuel and Kings, all of which underwent redaction after the Babylonian Exile before reaching their present form. It is worth noting that the Deuteronomistic accounts are written in late Mosaic Hebrew, which is different from the Hebrew of the post-exilic period (Finkelstein and Silberman 2007, p. 263).

The Book of the Law became the definitive code, whose strict laws and observances would define the survival of the people of Israel in their exile. The people felt reassured that King Josiah would remove the abominations of their neighbors, reinstitute the laws of the Bible, and bring back the past glory that had been preserved in legends. The ethical approach, the support for human rights, and the dignity of the Book of the Law appealed to all citizens, especially the numerous poor. Jerusalem under the subsequent reforms reached a new height in its standard of living that would not be achieved again until the Roman period in the 1st century CE.

Much later Biblical scholars realized that there was a strong parallel between the Book of the Law and Deuteronomy, and that the two versions had been combined. It is safe to say that the account of Josiah's discovery of a scroll gives credence to the writing of the book of Deuteronomy in the 7th century BCE. However, the recounting of how the scroll was discovered has no basis in archaeological or historical fact.

During the reign of Josiah, the Assyrians withdrew from the area of Judah and radical change took place. Dreams of renewal, independence, and an opportunity to develop their own culture spread across the country. The possibility of bringing the Northern Kingdom back into a single monarchy gripped the local population. The first order of business was to destroy the altar at Beth El and to restore sanctity to the Jerusalem Temple, and then to bring the north under the moral and religious standards of Judah in the south.

In I Kings 13:2 an unknown Judahite prophet proclaims: "Behold a child shall be born to the house of David, Josiah by name." No clear archaeological evidence has been found to confirm the messianic role that Josiah was fulfilling in the Davidic tradition, or the notion that Deuteronomistic history was revealed to him. The priests played an important role in formulating the bulk of Deuteronomy. They made sure that all the layers of legends and historical memory were recorded as described to them in the first four books of the Bible.

With the discovery of the Deuteronomic scroll, the scribes became intent on retaining the Jacob legend, in which the twelve sons of Jacob are the progenitors of the twelve tribes. The frequent references to tribes in the Bible tell us that Israelite society had been tribalized in the past. As mentioned earlier, Israel and Judah grew out of a coalescing of various indigenous peoples. It seems that there were two different systems of organizing the tribes that were edited together into the scheme of the twelve tribes, a later development likely to have been created for ideological purposes (Grabbe 2007, p. 107). This consolidation could have taken place during the reign of Josiah. "Archaeological surveys have confirmed that many of the Bible's geographical lists—of the towns and villages of the tribes, of the districts of the kingdom—closely match settlement patterns and historical realities in the 8th and 7th centuries BCE" (Finkelstein and Silberman 2007, p. 263).

Although Josiah's reforms were primarily religious, they were also based on economics as he was attempting to create a greater Israel (Grabbe 2007, p. 204). The archaeological record of Josiah's reign is quite thin. Seals and seal impressions of late Judahite officials and dignitaries minimally provide the only evidence for Josiah's reforms. A Hebrew inscription is the earliest archaeological evidence. It appears on a shard (ostraca) from an unknown servant who was appealing for his human rights concerning a garment that was taken. He was demanding its return, which was interpreted as a new right protected by Deuteronomic law (Finkelstein and Silberman 2002, pp. 287-288).

Archaeological evidence for Josiah's reign and his role in the interface of the material finds and the Biblical account is also lacking. R.E. Friedman (1989, pp. 111-113) compares Josiah with Moses specifically during Josiah's reign when he was responsible for the seventh book of the Bible. Only two people, Moses and Josiah, are mentioned in the Biblical narrative as unparalleled. In addition, the command to "love Yahweh, your God with all your heart and with all your soul and with all your might" (Deuteronomy 6:15) is only expressed when Moses speaks to the people, and again by Josiah as "a king who returned to Yahweh with all his heart and with all his soul and with all his might" (II Kings 23:25). Both Moses and Josiah turn to Yahweh through a priest or a judge in difficult times. Also, the phrase "do not turn right or left to what is told of you" is only applied to Josiah (II Kings 22:2). The book "of the Torah" is mentioned only in Deuteronomy and not again, except in relation to Josiah (Deuteronomy 31:26 and II Kings 22:8). Furthermore, the public reading of the book of the Covenant in II Kings 23:2 is very close to Moses' oration of the law as described in Deuteronomy.

Josiah died by the hand of Necho II of the Twenty-sixth Egyptian dynasty. Two different versions of Josiah's encounter with Necho II at Megiddo are found in II Kings 23:29 and II Chronicles 35:23, both attesting to Josiah having been shot with an Egyptian arrow and dying. This episode is disputed, and Josiah may in fact have been executed by Necho II. These texts were translated from the Hebrew into Greek centuries later and use the name Armageddon for Megiddo. It was Josiah's death in 609 BCE that gave rise to the tradition that Megiddo is where the forces of good and evil will, some time in the future, do battle on the site where Josiah, the last Davidic king perished. Thus, the traditions of Judeo-Christian eschatology and Davidic messianism were born (Finkelstein and Silberman 2007, p. 207).

The great reforms initiated by Josiah, both religious and economic, collapsed after his death in 609 BCE. The population once again came under the rule of Egypt. The next four kings, three of them the sons of Josiah, presided over a period of decline, leading to the collapse and destruction of the Judahite state.

Despite all the praise lavished on Josiah by the priestly scribes, he is only known from Biblical sources. There are no references to him in contemporary Egyptian or Babylonian texts, and although we are nearing the point of relying on the Biblical text for historical credibility, we can only document his existence with limited archaeological evidence.

Chapter Eight

Redacting the Bible

The Babylonian Exile to Ezra

In 1982, the writer met with Gabi Barkai, professor of archaeology at Bar-Ilan University. Archaeological Seminars Institute had supplied a number of volunteers for Barkai's excavation at Ketef Hinnom, on the shoulder of the hill overlooking the Old City of Jerusalem. This site is directly under the Scottish Church of St. Andrew and across from the Jerusalem Cinematic. During our conversation, Barkai carefully opened a matchbox and unwrapped two silver cylinders with what appeared to be scratches on their exteriors. The markings were later identified as being "Yud Hey Vav Hey," the ancient Hebrew name for God. At the time, Barkai was investigating how to unroll these scrolls without causing them to disintegrate.

That process took three years of painstaking work at the University of Southern California's West Semitic Research Project laboratories, using advanced technology and computer-based enhancement techniques. The resulting data gave a dating of 600 BCE, or just prior to the destruction of Jerusalem by the Babylonians in 586 BCE. When the two scrolls were opened, the Priestly Blessing was revealed in both of them: "May YHWH bless you and keep you; may YHWH cause his face to shine upon you and grant you peace" (Numbers 6:24-26). This blessing is recited daily in the Jewish prayer book. This discovery represents the earliest interface of the Biblical account and an archaeological find (Figure 8.1).

The scrolls were probably worn as amulets to keep evil spirits away. They were found in a collapsed tomb on the hillside in an area that had no intrusions, and came to light as the result of a fallen roof on burial chamber #25. More than 1,000 material finds were found in the accumulated material, which was approximately 24 inches deep. The tomb in which the cylinders were found had been used continuously from about 650 BCE until a short time after the Babylonian destruction in 586 BCE. This date is consistent

75

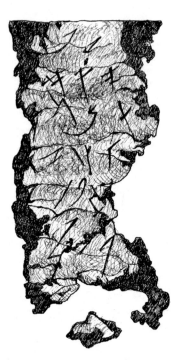

Figure 8.1. Cylinder amulet, Ketef Hinnom: hammered silver with words from the Priestly Blessing. Jerusalem, 6th century BCE.

with the view that the compilation of the Bible began no later than the time of King Josiah's reforms, which were connected to the discovery of the Book of the Law, Deuteronomy.

King Nabopolassar, the founder of the Neo-Babylonian empire, was succeeded in 604 BCE by his son Nebuchadnezzar II, called the Chaldean. His full name recalls the name mentioned in connection with Abraham in the Biblical text, nearly 1,000 years earlier. Abraham, according to the Biblical account, came from Ur "of the Chaldees," although the Chaldean empire was not in existence until the end of the 7th century BCE. Nebuchadnezzar drove the Egyptians out of Syria and concentrated his efforts on the beautification of his capital city Babylon with such projects as the Hanging Gardens. While excavating in the area of the Hanging Gardens, a cache of approximately 200 tablets was uncovered. Four of the tablets refer to the rations of grain and oil supplied by Jehoiachin, king of Judah. This is confirmed by the Babylonian Chronicles in 597 BCE when Nebuchadnezzar makes a token assault on Jerusalem and takes the king, his mother, and his family captive, along with 10,000 others, including the aristocracy and the priests (II Kings 24:12-14). But that was only the beginning of the slide to destruction! Nebuchadnezzar replaced Jehoiachin with his uncle, Zedekiah. Zedekiah rebelled and the Babylonian army began the siege of Jerusalem. The outlying areas fell to the Babylonian army. The book of Jeremiah (34:7) notes that Lachish and Azekah were the last cities in Judah to fall, while II Kings (25:3-7) describes the capture of Zedekiah as well as the murder of his sons in his presence. The Babylonians then put out Zedekiah's eyes and took him into exile in Babylonia. Jerusalem was left desolate.

The book of Ezra was originally combined with the writing of Nehemiah. As one volume, they first appeared around 440 BCE, approximately 150 years after the decree of Cyrus encouraging the Judeans to return to their homes. The books of Ezra continued to be revised until the 1st century CE. It has been suggested that the text was originally three sections put together by three different authors, and indeed the book's themes are the return to Zion in 538 BCE after the Babylonian captivity; the rebuilding of the Temple in Jerusalem in 515 BCE; and the rebuilding of the walls of Jerusalem by Nehemiah. It has been questioned whether Ezra himself wrote the text, or if it was done by the author or authors of Chronicles; alternatively, Ezra may have written both books. Is it possible that it was Ezra who assembled the five sources into the books of Moses (the Pentateuch) as we know them today? According to R. E. Friedman in *Who Wrote the Bible?* (1989, pp. 218-239), Ezra is the most likely of all the Aaronid priests to have had access to priestly documents such as the Book of Generations, a text focusing on name lists and genealogy. He may have structured the book of Genesis using priestly terminology and added the ending while in exile in Babylon or after the construction of the Second Temple. Certainly it was during the Second Temple period that the Aaronid priests were in authority. The stature of the priests in society at the time allowed them to establish and interpret the Bible. They were the main authority during this period, as there was no viable monarchy. The division between the Levites and the priests had already been established during the reign of King Hezekiah. Neither Biblical accounts nor archaeology have much to contribute about the period following the destruction of 587 BCE.

Kings and Chronicles conclude with the fall of Judah and the desolation of Jerusalem. There is no archaeological confirmation regarding the length of time the city was deserted. How then did those in exile remain loyal to their traditional homeland? Could the repeated recitation of the religious laws and observance of their strict dietary laws have kept them separate from the Babylonians? Other exiled peoples in Babylonia blended into their new location, as their gods were similar to the gods of the conquering nation. However, the religious laws of the Israelites were distinct, even restrictive, and incompatible with the other religions, which in turn helped to create a bridge for the return to Jerusalem.

The literary and historical traditions of the Israelites were reshaped in Babylon. Written accounts of the past were framed in terms of the present, to construct a pattern of history influenced by their captivity and separation from Jerusalem. The scribes and redactors during this period had an enormous influence on the formation of Israelite tradition, since it was they who put their people's earliest memories into literary form during the Babylonian Exile.

The death of Nebuchadnezzar in 562 BCE left his son Nabonidus (556-539 BCE) in charge of the already weakened Babylonian empire. Belshazzar, the next in line, was serving as regent when Cyrus the Great of Persia and his army walked into the city of Babylon unopposed. In archaeological excavation, no level of destruction has been found at this time. This event is recorded in Akkadian cuneiform script on the Cyrus Cylinder, which is in the British Museum (Figure 8.2). Cyrus had a quick rise to power and by 550 BCE he was the ruler of the Medes. He quickly showed his theological liberalism by returning the Israelite captives to their homeland, an event that is also recorded on the Edict of Restoration. In 538 BCE Cyrus ordered the return of the community and religious life to Jerusalem (Ezra 6:34).

According to the books of Ezra and Nehemiah, the Israelite population returned from captivity to Jerusalem led by Sheshbazzar and Zerubbabel, who became the leaders of the community. Jerusalem was a Persian province or satrapy at this time. By the time of Ezra most of the material included in the Bible had already been attributed to the tradition of Moses by the scribes. If Ezra was a primary redactor his main task was to retain as much of the original text as possible without too much contradiction so as not to disillusion the community. At the same time, he had to appease the priests by not diminishing their part in the narrative as he wove the stories together. The redacted

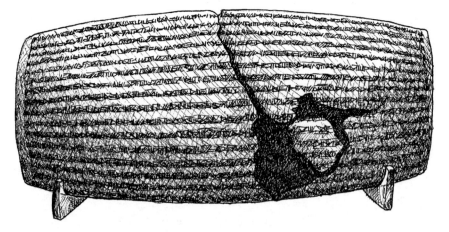

Figure 8.2. Cyrus Cylinder: baked clay with Akkadian cuneiform script. Contains a decree returning deported captives to their homelands, 6th century BCE.

texts were diverse and complicated, and yet there seems to be a meaningful organization. If Ezra was not the redactor, then he probably had a large part in the process and he is acknowledged by most scholars as a prime contributor in the redaction of first five books of Moses (Friedman 1989, p. 223-225).

Previously it was thought that the Babylonian Exile was almost total, emptying Judah of its populations between 586 and 538 BCE, and that only the poorest people stayed behind. However, I Kings 24:14 uses the number 10,000 to count the exiles and then two chapters later says that 8,000 Judahites went into exile. The prophet Jeremiah recounts three deportations of 46,000 (Jeremiah 52:28-30). Accordingly, it is now estimated that only 5% to 20% of the population was deported to Babylonia. Most of the people, especially those from rural areas, were not removed, and the exiles came mainly from Jerusalem and its environs. This was the area called Yahud, comprised mainly of the Judean hills. The boundaries of the area can be reconstructed archaeologically by the seal impressions with the name Yahud. Several hundred of these have been found in Jerusalem and at sites within 15 to 20 miles to the north and south of the city. It is from the word Yahud that the name Yehudim or Jews was derived. Yahud remained under Persian control for two centuries, until the conquest of Alexander the Great in 332 BCE (Finkelstein and Silberman 2002, p. 315).

The merger of the Biblical account and the archaeological remains becomes more compatible and reliable towards the end of the Biblical narrative. By the end of the 6th century BCE, the methods of recording events are in place and people are more literate. The Greek writer Herodotus (484-420 BCE) is considered to be the Father of History. The time in which he worked parallels the time of Ezra. It seems serendipitous that these two figures were active at the same time in the Mediterranean area. Herodotus is credited with the idea of recording events so that future generations can learn from the past. Ezra is remembered because, more than any other scribe, he seems to have crafted the guidelines that kept the Biblical narrative viable until the present time. The notion that Ezra was responsible for redacting the Bible is conjecture and not based on archaeological evidence.

After the reconstruction of the Second Temple in 515 BCE, Jerusalem began to emerge from its destruction of fifty years earlier, to become part of the newly configured Persian province. The return of Nehemiah, a high-ranking official in the court of the Persian king, marked the beginning of new construction for the city. Nehemiah negotiated with the king to allow the rebuilding of the city walls and was given a special document permitting the work to be completed. He involved the entire community in this project and within 50 days the work was finished The day of the dedication of the new walls was marked with joyous ceremony and marked the end of the Babylonian Exile.

Two hundred years later, Alexander the Great conquered the Persian empire in 332 BCE and assimilated the Persian holdings into the Hellenistic world. This confrontation between Western civilization and the Middle East was a traumatic event. Hellenism with its new religion and way of life swept away the local traditions. The books of Maccabees I through IV are considered the most reliable historical accounts and are considered by Jews and Protestants to be part of the Biblical apocrypha. The impact of Hellenism on Judaism led to the Maccabean revolt from 164-163 BCE, the Hasmonean kingship, and the rededication of the Temple in Jerusalem.

The Heliodorus Stele, recovered in 2005 by Ian Stern and Bernard Alpert on behalf of Archaeological Seminars Institute and the Israel Antiquities Authority at Tel Maresha, confirmed these events (Figure 8.3). This is the largest stele ever found in Israel and is dated to 178 BCE. The inscription, carved on limestone in Attic Greek, contains 28 lines, representing three pieces of correspondence. The most important is a royal exchange between King Seleucus IV (brother to Antiochus IV of the Hanukkah story), his chief minister Heliodorus, and two other officials. Initially the king was quite lenient with the

Figure 8.3. Heliodorus Stele, Tel Maresha: Attic Greek on limestone. Provides context for the Hanukkah story, 178 BCE.

community of Judah, but around 178 BCE he sent Heliodorus to Jerusalem to obtain money that was needed to pay Roman levies. Heliodorus entered the Temple and confiscated monies from its treasury. This act caused a great amount of tension and was one of the catalysts that sparked the Maccabean revolt in 175 BCE (II Maccabees chapter 3). The Heliodorus Stele thus provides credibility for the Hanukkah story which has been clouded in myth and legend (Stern, *Near Eastern Archaeology* 72:1 pp. 60-61).

It was during the reign of Herod the Great (37– 6 BCE), who ruled as a client king with Roman permission, that Jerusalem reached the height of its greatness and influence, only to be destroyed along with the Temple by Roman legions in 70 CE.

Nearly two thousand years have passed and the Bible remains as important as it was when it was redacted. From a modern perspective, getting the Bible together must be done with intellectual integrity, critical Biblical analysis, archaeological and scientific evidence, and humility. The work, inspired by respect for the tradition and knowledge of religion, requires immediate attention. New examination is needed, even if it contradicts the fundamentalist view of the Bible. The goal of reconciling the interface of Biblical narrative with archaeological evidence is in our reach.

It ain't necessarily so, but it is necessary!

Chapter Nine

Educational Perspectives
A Postscript

The Bible is taught in a variety of settings: adult education classes, Great Books seminars, and in synagogue and church schools. It is in these forums that questions concerning the truth of the Bible are frequently raised. Many students come to the table with preconceived ideas that may have been learned from their parents, or with attitudes of disbelief. While most are open to honest and non-biased discussions about all other subjects, when we look at the Biblical text there is often a tendency to become wary of what the material is asking us to hear. Educators present their material fairly in other subjects such as history, literature, and mathematics. In those fields of study, there is not much room for playing with the basics: a math equation is just that . . . a set of numbers, a literary classic is as it was when it was written, and historical data may be off by a year or two, but the events of the world are pretty clearly identified. But when we turn to religion we encounter much more in the way of personal prejudice and, ironically, the unwillingness or the inability to question long-standing points of view.

Entering the 21st century and addressing the issues of the postmodern world, educators, especially religious educators, are faced with a huge challenge. How do we continue to educate and mold religious and intellectually honest adherents of the three major faiths and at the same time honor our shared heritage?

What is needed is a re-evaluation of what we want to see as the result of our young people's introduction to formal religious education. If the goal is pride in their identity as Protestants, Catholics, Jews or Muslims, then we must convey honest information in interesting ways. We want our youth to walk out of religious schools equipped to meet the world with confidence and knowledge. The "how" is not difficult . . . we have many fine teachers who can present information with love and honesty. What is lacking is a clear sense that NOW is the "when" to start teaching the truth. The role of the educator is to teach students to think critically. There are multiple truths, and the decision of which truth to follow often depends on clearly presented information.

Opening a new vista on the Biblical text is a challenge, both for the adult learner and the young pupil. This is especially crucial in the after-school and Sunday educational programs. The average student in an American synagogue or church after-school program is the recipient of stories from the Hebrew or Christian Bible as they relate to major events or holidays. Jewish students learn enough Hebrew and information about Israel to get them through their bar or bat mitzvahs. In most cases, the failure rate is high and, in terms of understanding the issues raised in the Bible, most are still wandering in the desert.

The intense work of the archaeological community over the last six decades begs us to stop introducing Abraham, Isaac, and Jacob as if they walked the sands of the Middle East. That archaeological record mandates us to see these figures as paradigms for all that is engaging in Judaism and its daughter religions of Christianity and Islam. The Bible has given us a code of behavior that is applicable to the 21st century: lessons in morality, truth, social justice, and kindness that will improve our individual lives, help repair our troubled world, and reinforce the concept of a supreme creative force in our lives.

However, archaeological evidence is not enough to initiate a new point of departure in education. Many factors since the mid-20th century have also played a part in setting the stage for change in our educational institutions. Organized religion has been transformed since the end of World War II. Independent, thoughtful individuals who seek a more spiritual, open approach to text within a religious framework have been influenced by the women's movement, by the high-level education in religious day schools and camps, and by resurgence in spirituality using music and prayer. Independent prayer groups are established to meet new demographic needs, while alternative congregations of all types are more widely accepted. From young parents to baby boomers, people who are not afraid to fail, who pray with other hard-working, creative men and women, who are more affluent, are determined to make a difference in the world in a religious sense. This phenomenon is found in the Christian and Jewish denominations, as well as in the Islamic community of the West.

Like our parents and siblings, our grandparents, even great-grandparents whom we may never have met, we are all part of a larger family. Abraham, Isaac, and Jacob, his sons, and their children are all part of this enterprise, an extended family of cousins. We may not know much about them, and what we do know was written by other cousins many years later. Like any other family, story-telling becomes a large part of our heritage. Since photographs are limited to the last hundred-plus years, the stories we tell become the arena for painting word pictures of who is who in our family. Retelling the adventures of great-great-grandparents Hannah and Isaac, or Maria and Pablo as they made their way to America from Poland, Italy, or Mexico, create deep connections between those long-gone generations and our children's children today. In the same way, Abraham, Isaac, Jacob, and Moses represent our collective ancestors. They are the history of each religious or ethnic persuasion and we may be inclined to believe that they really lived as the Bibles describes. But, after many retellings, even the youngest child will question their reality while grasping the concepts they represent.

Gary Greenberg says:

> Precisely because the Bible has occupied so central a place in Jewish and Christian thought and life, it is the most difficult text to teach this narrative to our children. Time and usage have bestowed upon many of the past generations interpretation of the Bible sanctity almost equal to that attached to the text itself. Moreover, the book of Genesis in particular is replete with stories told to six and seven year old children in both Christian and Jewish religious schools, and has left the widespread impression that this book was written primarily for the entertainment of youngsters. Since very few students continue their religious studies long enough to be exposed to a more mature understanding of what Genesis is seeking to tell us, it remains in their minds, even after they grow up, as a collection of mildly interesting fairy tales (1974, p. xiv).

One of those tales is about the giving of the five books of Moses, a story that we read regularly. The Bible tells us that the Commandments were given by the God of Abraham, Isaac, and Jacob . . . but we don't really know exactly where Mount Sinai was or when God told the Jews about this gift. Was it really on a mountain, or is that part of an ancient tradition that associates major inspirational moments with high places? Many great religious ideas in other traditions have come from the gods on high. These ideas, in turn, were written down by wise men and women, when writing became prevalent. Oral traditions are often distorted over centuries of retelling, and the last version was probably codified much later, becoming the tradition we know today. There is no testing of their stories against the archaeological record.

The typical child, outside of an intensive parochial school setting, spends four to six hours a week learning the basic skills to prepare for his life as a member of a specific religious community. Various coming-of-age ceremonies such as first communion, confirmation, and bar and bat mitzvahs, are observed with great fanfare and then the 12- or 13-year-old adolescent is cut loose, as high school looms large on his or her personal horizon. Whatever basic information was absorbed in religious school is pushed aside in favor of the acquisition of knowledge needed to get into colleges and universities.

Religious education and Bible study fall by the wayside as students focus on their "real" future. Failure to educate these young individuals at the time that they are ready to understand philosophical subtleties (according to Piaget, the leading authority on child development) can have serious consequences. A certain level of maturity is required to understand the messages of ethical monotheism, rituals, and observation of the Sabbath and holidays. The emerging adult whose religious education is terminated at the most simplistic level will be hard-pressed to appreciate his heritage and is likely to remain unaware of being part of a peoplehood in an evolving religious civilization.

The challenge is how to educate our children to be informed adult members of religious communities? This is especially important if early adolescence marks the end, and not the beginning, of religious education. From the ages of five to ten years old, students are fed simplified Bible stories, songs, and art projects relating to basic holiday concepts and rudimentary methods of observance. Just when young minds are ready to grapple with serious basic texts and more complex ideas, they leave the educational framework of the extended religious community and go out into the world. Often, their earliest experiences have been less than satisfying. They have fallen victim to the after-school paradigm of 4 to 7 PM classes that follow a full day of secular school, where younger, talented instructors go hand in hand with modern technology. Children lap up data and thrive on the interactive approaches available in today's educational settings as they prepare for their future lives. When they are dropped off at the church or synagogue school, they are already tired; after a hurried snack, faced with repetitious litanies of Bible stories and holiday observances, they are turned off, not on!

Educators and parents need to come together to develop curriculum that is cognizant of the developmental stages of children so that the move to critical thinking is done at appropriate times and with maximum preparation. Piaget suggests the age of 12 as the time to teach abstract thinking. What better opportunity than the preparation for life-cycle events such as confirmation or bar and bat mitzvah to create seekers of truth through critical thinking, leaving the pediatric world of Bible stories and turning to the actual text.

If the Bible was written down in the 8th to 6th centuries BCE, as theorized by scholars from all points of the academic and religious compass, then it was probably formatted 400 years before the actual writing. That means that in the 12th to 10th centuries BCE the basic text of the Bible was beginning to take root. If we look at the current and accepted chronology of events in the Eastern Mediterranean, we see that the 13th to 12th centuries BCE is given as the date of the Exodus. What the confluence of the archaeological records and the text clarifies is that we may have to change this time frame, but not our belief system.

There are multiple truths and they are all valuable in our understanding of various individual religious points of view. Teaching this material as our valued heritage and the precepts and ethics we learn from the text is also holy work. This is not rejection of the Bible; it is gleaning the best of moral and literal truths from a time-honored text. Religion is not about exactly when things happened, but rather about what lessons we can learn from the text that can be incorporated into our daily lives.

Let's take a real issue. The Revelation at Sinai is a seminal event in the Bible. According to tradition, the Israelites received the Ten Commandments. What if Revelation never happened? Think about it this way: every day when we wake up and are alive is a great moment, a "revelation." Does that diminish the concept of a chosen people? And what of those Ten Commandments? Where would the world be without them? Why do we need them? This kind of frank and mind-opening questions posed by a qualified teacher to a middle-school class can spark discussion that will often highlight the students' basic quandaries and encourage attempts to answer their questions.

What factors and influences can be considered in the ethical dilemma as seen in this example? Can we consider Archaeology versus Revelation? Would a bit of research on the part of savvy 13-year-olds bring forth information on what the archaeological record has to say about Sinai, as well as passages that cite the giving of the law and the meaning of the Ten Commandments? How have these laws impacted the world over the past three millennia? What is the message on both sides of this discussion?

Questioning is part of childhood. From a toddler's first "what's that?" to the eight-year-olds' serious concern about who put the money under his pillow and took the tooth, parents and educators are giving answers that help to teach life's lessons. Amongst the hardest questions, the ones we all fear, are those that deal with God. Our oldest daughter always recited the traditional Jewish declaration of faith, the Shema, with her father at bedtime. The prayer declares, "Hear O Israel, the Lord our God, the Lord is one." When she was nearly three years old, she turned to her father and asked: "Daddy, when will God be two?" A perfectly natural question for a toddler, but a stumper for a parent or teacher who is not prepared. My husband may have said something like "God doesn't have a birthday like we do," but the question is more important than the answer. By the age of nine or ten, that same child might reject the bedtime ritual because it's hard to believe your earlier concepts of God, especially if there was an absorbing film about the Origin of the Species in science class.

The questions get harder as the child matures. The simple answers don't work and we, as parents and educators, need clearer responses. We speak of God in anthropomorphic terms which "lower" God to an old man with a grey beard in heaven, who is busy doing all the things the Bible tells us . . . creating the world, sending the Flood, splitting the sea, dropping manna in the desert, giving laws to Moses on Mount Sinai. For youngsters this is the stuff of the good guy/bad guy films they see on TV, but for adolescents and young adults, it has lost its luster and is boring at best.

Just as addition and subtraction are taught before multiplication, so too is it essential that we provide the building blocks needed to construct a belief system. A literal reading of the Bible will not result in deep faith for students who have grown up in the past decade and have internalized some measure of critical thinking. The questions they are asking are not "either/or." They are "and/also" questions . . . sincere inquiries that deserve sincere answers.

Who wrote the Bible and what does it have to do with us today? Is it important to accept that the Bible was given to us and written for us by God? Or can we say that Moses was divinely inspired and wise men and women wrote these oral inspirations years later? Farther afield is the notion that none of it happened as it was written, and that the Bible was based on different characters who had similar experiences at a different time. The important point here is not whether the text is truth, legendary or mythic. What is important is that we communicate that the Bible is a very special book, in a class by itself. It is not Harry Potter, Greek myths, or any other favorite story book. We can treasure all of these in their own right. But the Bible is a holy text, read by more people, for more years, more often, than any other book in the history of the world. The Bible has its own shelf and while commentaries continue to be written, it is still unchanged and unchallenged.

Why is it necessary to challenge it now? When young people of all faiths are looking for their own personal truth, when organized religion is under siege in many places, and traditional prayer services in churches and synagogues are seen as "uninspiring," why make a case for revamping our understanding of the Bible? It is precisely now, with Eastern religions, meditation and other exotic traditions vying for our attendance and attention, that we have to question our own practice and to consider 21st-century answers such as are found in this book.

God may be in his heaven but it is the work of man to make the world we live in a better place. Western religions hold to the idea that ethics begins with divine command and instruction, not as a product of human thought. We live by principles that direct our lives. These principles, in turn, become the framework that shapes our existence. While ethics is the foundation for proper behavior, the core of Biblical teaching is love of our fellow man as he was made in the image of God. That means that all of us are partners in creating a better world.

Who wrote the words in the Bible? It doesn't matter! What matters is what we do with those words in the 21st century.

Selected References

Aharoni, Yohanon. "The Israelite Occupation of the Canaan: An Account of the Archaeological Evidence." *Biblical Archaeological Review* (May/June 1982) 8:03.

Barth, Fredrik. *Ethnic Groups and Boundaries: The Social Organization of Culture Difference.* Little, Brown, 1969.

Bietak, Manfred. *Tell el-Daba.* University of Vienna, 1979.

Bowker, John. *Beliefs that Changed the World.* Quercus, 2007.

Bresler, Liora, David Cooper, and Joy Palmer, eds. *Fifty Modern Thinkers on Education.* Routledge, 2001.

Brettler, Marc Zvi. *How to Read the Bible.* Jewish Publication Society, 2005.

Cardin, Nina. *The Tapestry of Jewish Time.* Behrman House, 2000.

Chavalas, Mark W. and K. Lawson Younger, Jr., eds. *Mesopotamia and the Bible: Comparative Explorations.* Baker, 2002.

Cohen, Jack. *Jewish Education in Democratic Society.* Reconstructionist Press, 1964.

Currie, Robin and Stephen G. Hyslop. "The Letter and the Scroll: What Archaeology Tells Us about the Bible." *National Geographic,* 2009.

Curtis, Adrian. *Oxford Bible Atlas.* Oxford University Press, 2007.

Dever, W. G. "Western Cultural Tradition is at Risk." *Biblical Archaeology Review* 32 (2006), No. 2:26 and 76.

Dever, W. G. *What Did the Biblical Writers Know and When Did They Know It?* Eerdmans, 2002.

Dever, W. G. *Who Were the Early Israelites and Where Did They Come From?* Eerdmans, 2003.

Draper, Robert. "The Search for King David: New Discoveries in the Holy Land." *National Geographic* 218 (December 2010): 66-91.

Feiler, Bruce. *Walking the Bible.* Morrow, 2001.

Finkelstein, Israel. "Pots and People: Ethnic Boundaries in the Iron Age." *Journal for the Study of the Old Testament Supplemental Series* 237 (1997): 17-30.

Finkelstein, Israel and Amihai Mazar. *The Quest for the Historical Israel: Debating Archaeology and the History of Early Israel.* Society of Biblical Literature, 2007.

Finkelstein, Israel and N. A. Silberman. *The Bible Unearthed.* Simon & Schuster, 2002.

Finkelstein, Israel and N.A. Silberman. *David and Solomon.* Free Press, 2007.

Fishbane, M. A. *Biblical Interpretation in Ancient Israel.* Clarendon Press, 1985.

Fox, Seymour, Israel Scheffler, and Daniel Marom, eds. *Visions of Jewish Education.* Cambridge University Press, 2003.

Friedman, R. E. *Who Wrote the Bible?* Harper Collins, 1989.

Gitin, Seymour and T. Dotan. *Tel Miqne-Ekron 1981-1996.* Albright Institute and Hebrew University, 2005.

Golden, J. M. *Ancient Canaan and Israel.* Oxford University Press, 2004.

Gottwald, Norman K. *The Tribes of Yahweh: A Sociology of the Religion of Liberated Israel 1250-1050 BCE.* Sheffield Academic Press, 1999.

Grabbe, L. L. *Ancient Israel.* T. T. Clark, 2007.

Greenberg, Gary. *101 Myths of the Bible.* Sourcebooks, 2002.

Halpern, Baruch. *Text and Artifacts: Two Monologues* (Archaeology of Israel). Sheffield Academic Press, 1997.

Hertz, J. H. *Pentateuch and Haftorahs.* Soncino Press, 1979.

Herzog, Ze'ev. "Historical Accuracy of the Bible Called into Question." *Ha'aretz* newspaper, October 29, 1999, Tel Aviv.

Hoffmeier, James K. *The Archaeology of the Bible.* Lion, 2008.

Horwitz, Liora Kolska and others. *Dan I: A Chronicle of the Excavation, the Pottery Neolithic, the Early Bronze Age and Middle Bronze Age Tombs.* Hebrew University. 1966-7; 1986.

Kaunfer, Elie. *Empowered Judaism.* Jewish Light Publishing, 2010.

Keller, Werner. *The Bible as History.* Barnes & Noble, 1995.

Kugel, James L. *How to Read the Bible.* Simon & Schuster, 2007.

Levine, Lee. "Biblical Archaeology (Etz Hayim Tanach)." *Jewish Publication Society of America,* 1995.

Magnusson, Magnus. *The Archaeology of the Bible Lands.* Bodley Head, 1997.

Mazar, Ami. "Excavations at Tel Beit Shean." *Biblical Archaeology Today* (1990): 150-163.

Mendelson, Alan. *Secular Education in Philo of Alexandria.* Hebrew Union College Press, 1982.

Meshel, Ze'ev. *Sinai: Excavations and Studies.* British Archaeological Reports, 2000.

Narkiss, Bezalel. *Picture History of Jewish Civilization.* Massada Ltd, 1978.

Neill, A. S. and others. *Summerhill: For and Against.* Hart Publishing Company, 1970.

Neusner, Jacob. *The Talmud: What It Is and What It Says.* Rowman & Littlefield, 2006.

Piaget, Jean and others. *The Growth of Logical Thinking from Childhood to Adolescence.* Basic Books, 1958.

Redford, Donald B. *Egypt, Canaan, and Israel in Ancient Times.* Princeton University Press, 1993.

Sarna, Nahum M. *Understanding Genesis.* Schocken, 1970.

Schofield, J. N. *The Historical Background of the Bible.* Thomas Nelson and Sons, 1946.

Schulweis, Harold M. *Conscience: The Duty to Obey and the Duty to Disobey.* Jewish Light Publishing, 2008.

Sewell, Curt. "The Tablet Theory of Genesis Authorship." *Bible and Spade* 1 (1994).

Shibutani, T. and K. M. Kwan. *Ethnic Stratification.* Macmillan, 1965.

Smith, Evans Lansing and Nathan Robert Brown. *The Complete Idiot's Guide to World Mythology.* Penguin, 2007.

Stager, L. "Why Were Hundreds of Dogs Buried at Ashkelon?" *Biblical Archaeology Review* 17 (1991): 27-42.

Wapnish, Paula. "Camels, Caravans and Pastoralists at Tel Jemmah." *Janes* (1981).

Wapnish, Paula. "Pig's Feet, Cattle Bones and Birds' Wings." *Biblical Archaeology Review* 22 (1996).

Woolley, Leonard and P. R. S. Moorey. *Ur 'of the Chaldees': A Revised and Updated Edition of Sir Leonard Woolley's Excavations at Ur.* Cornell University Press, 1982.

Yerushalmi, Yosef Hayim. *Zakhor: Jewish History and Jewish Memory.* University of Washington Press, 2005.

About the Authors

Bernard and Fran Alpert have lived in Jerusalem for 31 years. Bernard has excavated at Damascus Gate, the Citadel of David, the Gate of the Essenes, and the Western Wall area of the Temple Mount and Ketef Hinnom in Jerusalem, as well as the Winter Palace at Herodion and Herod's Summer Palace at Jericho. For the past twenty years he has been excavating as one of the chief archaeologists at Beit Guvrin-Tel Maresha in co-operation with the Israel Antiquities Authority and the Israel Nature and Parks Authority. Fran is a well-known guide, with extensive experience in Israel and Jordan, and an engaging lecturer on the archaeology and history of Jerusalem. She is also the author of *Getting Jerusalem Together*, a guide to the antiquities of Jerusalem which has sold more than 20,000 copies.

Founders of Archaeological Seminars Institute, the Alperts have been able to evaluate firsthand the benefit of an inquiry-based approach to understanding Israel. Dig for a Day, their innovative excavation program, has given more than one million participants the opportunity to study and learn by taking part in an ongoing archaeological excavation. Archaeology has come alive for them, not only through the dig process, but also with interactive walking tours, seminars, and study courses offered for nearly three decades by Archaeological Seminars Institute. The Alperts' unique educational approach to tourism has been widely praised.

Fran and Bernard Alpert hold Master's degrees in Classical Archaeology from Oxford University/Wolfson College. They have lived in Israel since 1979, holding dual US and Israeli citizenship.